'Having spent millions of dollars and thousands of hours in developing database marketing machinery, tools and automated techniques, our industry finds itself technology tired, number numb and not one step closer to the customer. McKean's insights have enabled us to move toward true information mastery and customer intimacy.'

Paul Rabideau, Director of Marketing Sciences, Novartis Corp

'McKean wastes no time in dissecting the real issues from the myths in terms of information competency and CRM. Without doubt, the time spent reading this book will prove invaluable for anyone striving to implement a coherent business and information strategy.'

Ewan Hutton, Business Development Manager, First Direct

'Every time we contact a customer, or they contact us, it's really a "moment of truth". By providing the right people and culture together with appropriate customer centric processes and an adult to adult dialogue, we can maximize on this event. Our data and technology should support this, not drive it. John's excellent book shows the route to this paradigm.'

Rob Strange, Change Programme Director,
Legal and General Assurance Co Ltd

'Too often, experts in this field can become besotted by technology and both customer and corporation needs become secondary issues. John McKean's book will no doubt draw some criticism from those who are offended with his pragmatism and realism; however, it is they who need to move from product and technology orientation, into a world where our customers share with the corporation, the value that world class excellence in Information Management can create. The balance between technology innovation and customer needs . . . should inspire all who follow this doctrine towards true mastery in Information Management.'

Michael Coomer, Chief Information Officer, National Australia Bank

'McKean provides an insightful and compelling framework in his book to help firms proactively avoid the easy trap of simply buying some technology, plugging it in and expecting the sun to come out, in their pursuit of better understanding and servicing customers.'

Roger Elwell, Head of Marketing and Product Development,
NatWest Card Services E-Commerce

'John has hit on the true essence of creating profitable customer relationships – balancing the information investments in the non-technological drives of effective service, quality, communications, reputation, and billing when applying information throughout the customer value chain.'

William H. Tallman, General Manager – Strategic Marketing,
GTE Wireless

'We have to move to the 'Market of One' and away from the tyranny of averages. John McKean demonstrates important insights into this most important strategy in this book.'

Michael Winch, Information Technology Director, Safeway Plc

'John McKean brings a keen intelligence to the real world business issues associated with data exploitation. This clear-headed analysis is valuable and refreshing in a market that has been infatuated for too long with the underlying technology.'

Sean Kelly, founder, The Data Warehouse Network

Information Masters

To my family who supported the writing of this book –
my mother Barbara, wife Martha, and daughter Jessica

And to the information visionaries whose bravery and
vision extended beyond the corporate realities of their time.

Information Masters

Secrets of the Customer Race

John McKean
Executive Director, Center for Information Based Competition

'. . . Less than five percent of the world's firms achieve the full potential of their customer relationship initiatives

. . . The rest are caught in its paradox . . .'

JOHN WILEY & SONS, LTD

Chichester • New York • Weinheim • Brisbane • Singapore • Toronto

Published 1999 by John Wiley & Sons Ltd,
Baffins Lane, Chichester,
West Sussex PO19 1UD, England

National   01243 779777
International (+44) 1243 779777
e-mail (for orders and customer service enquiries): cs-books@wiley.co.uk
Visit our Home Page on http://www.wiley.co.uk
                     or http://www.wiley.com

Reprinted September 1999

Other Wiley Editorial Offices

John Wiley & Sons, Inc., 605 Third Avenue,
New York, NY 10158-0012, USA

WILEY-VCH Verlag GmbH, Pappelallee 3,
D-69469 Weinheim, Germany

Jacaranda Wiley Ltd, 33 Park Road, Milton,
Queensland 4064, Australia

John Wiley & Son (Asia) Pte Ltd, 2 Clementi Loop #02-01,
Jin Xing Distripark, Singapore 129809

John Wiley & Sons (Canada) Ltd, 22 Worcester Road,
Rexdale, Ontario M9W 1L1, Canada

Library of Congress Cataloging-in-Publication Data

McKean, John, *1956–*
    Information masters : secrets of the customer
    race / John McKean.
        p.   cm.
    Includes index.
    ISBN 0–471–98801–4
    1. Customer relations.   I. Title
HF5415.5.M33   1999
658.8′12—dc21   99–13342
                                          CIP

British Library Cataloguing in Publication Data

A catalogue record for this book is available from the British Library

ISBN 0–471–98801–4

Typeset from the author's disks in 11/13pt. Plantin by Dorwyn Ltd, Rowlands Castle, Hants.
Printed and bound in Great Britain by Biddles Ltd, Guildford and King's Lynn
This book is printed on acid-free paper responsibly manufactured from sustainable forestry,
in which at least two trees are planted for each one used for paper production.

Contents

Preface

THIS BOOK IS ABOUT THE RACE BACK TO CUSTOMER INTIMACY by the leading firms in the world and their resulting information race.

The findings were gathered through interviews, trade publications, and public forums involving firms such as Abbey National Bank, ABN-AMRO, Advance Bank, Bank of America, Bank of Scotland, Barclays Bank, Barnett Bank, Chase Manhattan Bank, Commonwealth Bank of Australia, Dean Witter, Fidelity Investments, First Direct, Lloyds Bank, Legal & General, Midland Bank (HSBC group), National Australia Group, Nations Bank, PNC Bank Corp, National Australia Bank, NatWest, Royal Bank of Scotland, Royal Sun Alliance, Sainsbury's Bank, St. George Bank, Star Banc, Sun Trust, TSB, US Bancorp, Wells Fargo, VISA, American Drug Stores, Caldor, Casino, Elder Beerman, The GAP, Hallmark, K-Mart, Marks & Spencer, Meijer, Migros, Osco, J. Sainsbury, Sears, Tesco, W.H. Smith, Wal-Mart, AT&T, GTE, MCI, o.tel.o, Sprint, and US West.

The book candidly captures the success and failure of efforts to create customer information mastery in support of profitable customer relationships.

Of these firms, the leaders were able to balance today's powerful customer approaches with the information competencies required to execute them. They fought tremendous battles to change deeply rooted mass-market information legacies before ultimately achieving significant bottom-line impacts in areas such as marketing, sales, service, and loyalty. In the process of dragging their firms kicking and screaming toward information competency for the 21st century, they engaged almost every organism of profit and power within their firms before severing the tether to the mass markets of the 20th century.

The focus is on what actually happened as these firms tried to implement changes to mass-market customer information legacies to a customer-focused business model. This book documents the specific bottom-line payback and challenges experienced by these firms.

Acknowledgements

THIS BOOK SHARES THE EXPERIENCE OF FIRMS WHO ARE ON the road to customer information mastery – the race to become the world's foremost customer master.

The research consisted of some of the world's largest consumer intensive corporations, all of which had undertaken major customer information initiatives. The decision to withhold the names of firms in this book was made in order to provide an unfiltered view of the tempestuous ordeal of the struggle to build customer information competencies required by today's powerful customer approaches.

Thank you to the people who contributed their insight and observations of their firm's long-term efforts on the road to customer information mastery.

There were many people who contributed to the caliber of the research. Thanks to the cooperating firms who will remain nameless in this book for added confidentiality. The individuals and firms that dedicated their time, resources, and enthusiasm to this project deserve many thanks. Each participant added unique perspective to the research and its ultimate conclusions.

Special thanks for their thoughts, inspiration, efforts and support goes to Gary Abramson, Bob Barker, James Bauer, Peter Boulter, Erik Brynjolfsson, Jordan Byk, Gary Cameron, Doug Cheney, Sarah Cliffe, Kevin Condron, Henry Cook, Michael Coomer, Peter Drucker, Trevor Dukes, John Edwards, Roger Elwell, Richard Evans, Maggie Flynn, Jeffery Gersbach, Jim Goodnight, Ted Gorder, Peter Greis, Gary Hamel, Mike Haydock, John Henderson, George Hofheimer, Ewan Hutton, Glen Kaiser, Krystie Keller, Sean Kelly, Norm Kern, Ray Kordupleski, Philip Kotler, Robert Materna, Jose Maymo, Beverly McKean, Bruce McKean, Randy Mott, Kenneth Oppenheimer, David Overton, Don Peppers and Pamela Devenney,

John Peterson, Lisa Pope, Paul Rabideau, Frederick Reichheld, Robert Rose, Peter Sassone, Dave Schardt, Jeffrey Shoemacher, Matt Stankey, Bryan Stapp, Rob Strange, Dave Talbot, William H. Tallman, Scarlett Van Der Meulen, Irene Whitcomb, Michael Winch, Robert Wyllie, Jeremy Wyman, and the professional staff at John Wiley & Sons.

1

Customer Masters are Information Masters

THE CUSTOMER MASTERS ARE THE INFORMATION MASTERS.

They are not the high-profile firms that first come to mind.

They are not the firms touted by learned authors in the leading trade and business journals, nor do they publicly proclaim innovations in marketing, sales, customer loyalty, or technology.

On the contrary, they are the quiet ones.

They have a hushed appreciation for being on a steady trajectory toward the Holy Grail of business – to efficiently produce a win–win proposition for customers and shareholders simultaneously.

Their successes are deep, inconspicuous, and difficult to replicate by competitors.

They have achieved customer information mastery because of their recognition that customer functions such as marketing, sales, and service are not competencies themselves but strategies whose implementation is a component of a systemic information competency underpinning the entire firm.

Beyond this recognition is an awareness that information competency is primarily non-technological in nature and requires a balanced investment across the seven information competency determinants of people skills, processes, organization structure, culture, leadership, technology, and information itself.

As a result, the masters are acquiring and retaining the best customers and repelling the worst.

They are shrouded by their competitors' blindness.

They are quick and iterative.

They are obsessed with customers.

They are obsessed with information.

They are dangerous.

They are the future.

They are the Information Masters.

But they are the lucky ones.

The information masters represent roughly 5% of the world's firms who have achieved long-term success with customer relationship management. The rest are caught in its paradox.

They are the lucky ones in a business world increasingly driven by Hollywood business approaches and ever-accelerating technologies.

The corporate world, intoxicated by business gurus and technological advances, has desperately lurched toward quick fixes for waning customer loyalty and shrinking margins, as if the underlying causes of such ills would somehow magically resolve themselves through superficial antidotes.

Attentions have been focused on high-profile marketing, sales, and service functions rather than concentrating on the more difficult challenges of an underlying information competency upon which those functions rely.

Firms have looked toward technology to create the supporting information capabilities required by these customer-focused approaches, assuming that technology is the primary determinant of information competency.

This research clearly shows that technology is only one of the seven factors which determine information competency. Empirically, firms have applied 82% of the investment in their ability to apply information toward technology, yet technology only determines 10% of a firm's information competency.

Such myopia has only created further confusion and paradox, paralleling our non-business world.

In our non-business world are declining birth rates, yet ever-increasing population.

In our non-business world are record harvests, yet persistent hunger.

In our business world, there are technological advances for storing massive amounts of customer buying behavior, yet relatively less customer knowledge.

In our business world, there are radical technological advances to analyze customer information, yet customer loyalties spiral downwards.

Despite exponential technological advances, the complexities of our world have engulfed business in a flood of customer information far beyond the competency to use it.

We are not in the Information Age but in an age of information.

This lack of a true information competency has forced business to summarize and aggregate information about customer needs, behavior, and relative profitability.

This aggregation has produced detachment.

Detachment produced a culture.

The culture became tradition.

Both corporation and customer progressively became hardened to this emerging culture of remoteness and indifference.

As if to torment, the gurus of marketing, sales, service, and loyalty have offered intoxicating answers to our conundrum of the ever-distanced customer.

Their mesmerizing approaches offer sound strategy but executable success is continually restricted by one irrefutable fact.

Returning to the levels of intimacy and loyalty created by the quaint corner grocer under the burden of today's complexity and scale requires a broad and deep information competency far beyond what exists today in most firms.

In response, firms have quickly turned toward technology, believing that technological competency is the major determinant of information competency.

It is not.

Paradoxically, this unbalanced bias toward technology is only one small element of the predominantly non-technological determinants of information competency. Such non-technical elements range from an employee's skill to apply information to the willingness of business units to share information.

This unbalanced bias perpetuates the firm's underlying customer weakness, which in turn causes the firm to continue cycling through the following:

1 Competitive realization that firms need to get closer to our customers.

2 Expose themselves to all of the latest marketing, loyalty, and services approaches.

3 Attempt to implement those ideas and find that they all require a higher information competency.

4 They make major IT investments believing that this will create the required information competency.

5 The marketing, loyalty, and services initiatives make small gains but remain relatively anemic because IT is less than 10% of the information competency equation.

6 Because the major determinants of their information competency are non-technological and are the more difficult ones to address (people, process, organization, cultural, leadership, and information itself), they remain 'in the closet' and under-invested.

7 The firms cycle back to #2 and #4, i.e. pouring water into a leaky bucket.

This cycle drives firms to pour significant investments into tactical marketing, sales, service, and loyalty initiatives to address their weakness, which actually stems from an underlying weakness in information competency.

At the same time, firms continue to pour significant investments into information initiatives centered on technological capabilities in the belief that technology itself creates information competency.

As a result, marketing departments continue to perpetuate failure rate 'norms' from direct mail campaigns in the ninety percentiles while damaging brand and further alienating customers. Cost of customer loyalty incentives is on the rise. Sales departments experience continued productivity erosion, forcing cost reductions in core sales-support areas. Customer loyalty indicators show customer churn rates escalating toward 20–50% per year.

There are a number of firms who have broken free.

At the epicenter of these progressive firms is a handful of corporate heroes or 'information visionaries' whose corporate bravery and vision have propelled their firms beyond the riptide of legacy information approaches.

It is these visionaries who had the fortitude to run the rapids of corporate denial and drive their firm kicking and screaming into uncharted waters. The essence of their journey is eloquently captured by this Machiavellian wisdom: 'There is nothing more perilous to conduct, or more uncertain in its success, than to take the lead in the introduction of a new order of things, because the innovator has for enemies all those who have done well under the old conditions, and lukewarm defenders in those who may do well under the new'.

This is the story of their journey to information mastery.

The Customer Race is an Information Race

The firms who have made this perilous journey began with the understanding that unless a firm has fewer than one hundred customers, the race to acquire and retain the best customers is not a customer race but an information race.

Understanding customer needs and making decisions to profitably serve those needs is derived primarily (80–90%) from a firm's recorded information.

Therefore, the ability to apply this information is probably the single most important factor in acquiring and profitably serving customers and shareholders.

Yet, as firms were caught up in the latest frenzy of innovations to marketing, sales, and service, they continued to support these innovations with information by focusing on technological capabilities merely to tactically analyze and apply current information to specific initiatives.

This biased approach reveals that most firms view their ability to optimally apply customer, operational, and financial information as a technologically based proficiency rather than as a broad, underlying competency determined by elements ranging from employee information skills to business unit politics.

The typical firm invests in massive customer databases and networks without investing in the other elements which determine a true competency in information:

1   Employee skills to apply it.
2   Processes by which to efficiently deploy it.
3   Organizational structures and rewards for effective use in and across functional areas.
4   Culture to perpetuate the use and appreciation of its value.
5   Leadership to fully understand and support its role and investment.
6   Information itself relative to its value and accuracy.

Cart before the Horse

The inspiring goals of today's segment-of-one marketers, sales leaders, and customer loyalty gurus are possible only when firms first focus on developing a broad and deep information competency in support of such goals.

The firms who are well on their way to near information mastery levels have found that their previous efforts to implement segment-of-one marketing failed because they did not have systemic information competency to adequately execute the promises of segment-of-one marketing. They also came to realize that as they evolved their levels of information competency, they gained the inherent capability to implement segment-of-one marketing as a competency, not a tactical business initiative – a subtle but profound distinction.

The current obsession of many of the world's largest firms with executing a customer-focused business model without first addressing the information realities of complex and intimate customer approaches is premature.

For firms with less than one hundred customers, information competencies can exist more naturally within their business, as this environment is inherently less complex. As firms move beyond this number of customers, they are forced to proactively manage customer behavior in the context of operational efficiencies and financial performance in an increasingly complex environment. This complex business environment creates a dependency on the ability to apply massive amounts of detailed customer information in concert with operational and financial performance measures.

While many firms believe they are on a competitive trajectory for developed information competencies in support of customer-focused initiatives, their investments are biased toward technological investment rather than addressing the more difficult areas that represent the greatest inhibitors of creating customer and shareholder value for information.

The shortfall of a technologically based approach to information competency stems from the unresolved issues of business not looking beyond their narrow focus of their corporate database prowess, beyond the barriers of organizational agenda and politics, and beyond the information skills and processes optimized for business in yesteryear. This competency must exist at the heart of every breath the firm takes relative to creating value for customers and shareholders simultaneously.

The leading firms who have truly focused on the long-term development of information competencies in support of a customer-focused business model have achieved unparalleled levels of marketing effectiveness, sales performance, and customer loyalty.

Applying information to customer-focused business models continues only superficially in most firms, who take premature solace in their ability to apply information to current profitability, corporate databases or data warehouses. While most firms claim information competency, the results of their marketing and service initiatives prove they're getting only a fraction of their true potential.

While most have made some progress toward information competency, the concept of rich individual customer understanding
coupled with financial reality still does not exist for most firms
today. Instead, information is simply glorified record keeping and
administration rather than a profitable value-creation tool.

Much of this legacy has developed over years of informational
myopia; information was viewed as an operational necessity rather
than as the primary tool for creating value for customers and shareholders. Firms undervalue information because their ability to apply
it is so intertwined with and fundamental to every aspect of business
that it is simply taken for granted, and overlooked as a distinctive
competency.

A firm's information level may be ubiquitous to the point of
obscurity, yet it is the vehicle through which all other competencies
travel and the conduit through which all business initiatives must
pass. Ultimately, there is no business without information.

As we view the so-called Information Age, we find a world whose
information competency has not advanced but actually degraded
over the 20th century: for example, we accept that 97% of mailed
solicitations are unwanted, don't pay off, and are a source of consumer irritation. Although this particular statistic is currently considered an acceptable business norm, a business proprietor of one
hundred years ago would have considered this absurd.

The McKean Paradox

After studying many firms around the firm who had implemented
major information initiatives, a curious paradox was uncovered.
Most firms believed that the majority of drivers of information competency were technological, while the reality was that these drivers
were of a non-technological nature.

Operating under this false belief, a majority of firms have invested
in developing customer, operational, and financial information
capabilities with an unbalanced bias toward technological elements
rather than the non-technological elements of these capabilities,
which actually determined the majority of a firm's information
competency.

Table 1.1 reveals the paradox between the historical investments in customer information competencies by percentages compared to the actual customer information competency determinants.

Table 1.1   Historical investments vs. competency determinants

Elements	Historical Investment	Competency Determinants
People	2%	20%
Processes	2%	15%
Organization	2%	10%
Culture	1%	20%
Leadership	1%	10%
Information	10%	15%
Technology	82%	10%
TOTAL	100%	100%

Ironically, the firm's resources, which could have been reinvested more efficiently in the other six areas, were being consumed by downstream costs created by the very weakness of their own customer information competency.

Examples are:

✦ lowering prices to compensate for weaknesses in product competitiveness, rather than lower prices created by operational efficiencies;

✦ raising customer incentives to compensate for poor customer understanding;

✦ raising sales commissions because of poor marketing segmentation;

✦ increasing advertising to compensate for a weak value proposition;

✦ increasing the size of marketing campaigns to compensate for poor analysis;

✦ cutting support services because of poor sales resulting from poor targeting.

While the majority of the efficiencies in a balanced investment approach are long-term in nature, the reported short-term gains registered exponential ROIs.

The facts bore out the following conclusions:

1 The firm's view of information as a tactical support element rather than as the primary factor determining a firm's customer, operational, and financial decisions, drove the respective unbalanced investments in technology.

2 A firm's downstream weaknesses in areas such as customer loyalty, operational inefficiencies, and financial ambiguity consumed the firm's resources with reactionary fixes caused by an inherent information weakness.

3 This cycle perpetuated a narrow view, creating a narrow investment, and thus a low level of information competency.

The most brilliant strategies or initiatives in marketing, sales, customer service, and customer loyalty remained anemic when the other six elements of customer information competency did not have a balanced investment.

This anemia plays out in marketing departments who continue to generate failure rates from direct mail campaigns in the ninety percentiles. Cost of customer loyalty incentives is on the rise. Sales departments experience continued productivity erosion, forcing cost reductions in core sales support areas. Customer loyalty indicators show customer churn rates escalating in almost every industry by 5–25%.

Relative Customer Information Competency

The firms who ranked toward the very right hand portion of Figure 1.1 have a more balanced view and investment of customer information competency. As a result, most functional business areas score well above the industry norms.

A bird's eye view of the world's information competency reveals a competitive landscape diverse in its ability to apply customer, operational, and financial information effectively.

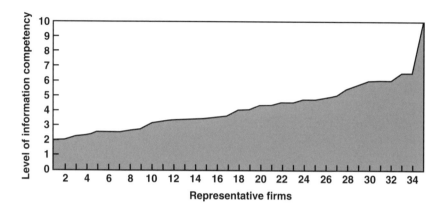

Figure 1.1   Relative customer information competency across industries

Observing over thirty-five of the world's leading firms who have implemented major customer information initiatives has revealed that most firms are ineffective in driving customer and shareholder value simultaneously, i.e. a consistent win–win proposition.

The small number of firms who ranked above five on a scale of one to ten showed a slightly more balanced view and consequently a more balanced investment in their customer information competency.

This slight difference has yielded unusually high financial returns as well as driving noticeable improvements in customer loyalty and churn rates.

The most striking accomplishment was that the firms who scored lower on the scale reported they sensed a subtle deterioration of their customer base, while the firms who scored relatively high had a much more detailed account of their customer-based improvement and their competitors' growing customer weakness.

In two sequential discussions between market competitors, the highly ranked firm described in excruciating detail the attributes of customers that they were surgically extracting from their lesser-ranked competition. The lower ranked competition described in approximate numbers the customers who were being stolen by their competitor but were quite vague as to their attributes and number.

The most striking difference between these groups was that the firms who ranked five and above who attacked the firms ranked five and below found these attacks largely undetected, leaving the lesser developed firms with an unrecognized deterioration of the customer base.

The select firms who approached information competency levels of 8–10 were as close as a firm could get in achieving a level of intimacy and loyalty reminiscent of the corner grocery store while operating at an exponential level of complexity.

Genetics of a Master

Of the leading firms studied around the world who have invested in major customer information initiatives, two-thirds of the firms have significantly unbalanced investments in their information competency. As a result, they are forced to compete in their market on short-term and tactical levels with their long-term profitability under siege.

One-third of the firms studied have started to gradually move in the direction of balancing their investments, which has directly impacted performance measures in the areas of marketing, sales, service, and loyalty.

Firms in the top of the top third had certain distinguishing characteristics.

The first is the culture of true customer focus.

Customer Obsession Necessitates Information Obsession

The information masters have a deep obsession for customers. Consequently, they are driven to a deep and quiet obsession for customer information in the context of operational efficiency and financial performance, i.e. information competency.

The genetics behind the information obsession:

1   Obsession with customers necessitates
2   Obsession with customer information, creates

3 Clarity as to the breadth and depth of true customer information competency, initiates

4 Investment in the broad range of elements which drive customer information competency:

— people skills;
— processes;
— organization structure;
— culture;
— leadership;
— information;
— technology.

All these elements must work in harmony to create customer information competency.

When one or more of these elements are inadequate, both customer and shareholders suffer.

Surgical Agility

The customer information masters serve customers with the precision of a surgeon.

This surgical agility enables them to:

✦ plunder the best customers through understanding them better and quicker;

✦ embrace their best customers through value rather than short-term incentives;

✦ teach the less profitable customers to interact more profitably;

✦ encourage their worst customers to patronize competitors;

✦ uncover profitable free agents.

The competitive effects of these surgical customer actions go largely undetected because their victim's lesser-developed customer information competencies mask the timing and size of impact.

In essence, the bottom-line impact creates a double jeopardy for competitors, resulting in a quiet shift in customer quality:

+ strengthening the customer base of the masters;
+ weakening the customer base of the competitors.

This double-edged attack is further compounded by the Pareto principles of customer value. The targeted shifts are focused on two segments:

+ the top 20% which drives 8% of the profits;
+ the bottom 20%, which drives 80% of the costs, e.g. fraud, abuse, bad debt, cost to service, churn.

Therefore, the customer information masters minimize the costs of services to customers, while generating a relatively high customer profit level.

Cloaked by Competitors' Weakness

The information master's subtle shifts in the value of their customer mix are difficult to detect.

If the competitors are fortunate enough to sense this subtle migration in customer quality, it is typically attributed to prowess in traditional business areas, i.e. good marketeering, a suave sales force, inherent customer loyalty. In most cases, the source behind the master's success is rarely attributed to systemic information competency.

Why is this so?

Concepts of traditional marketing, sales, or customer service are more readily understood and accepted as they are traditional business areas. In addition the concept of horizontal competencies, which underpin and traverse every functional area of business, is more difficult to assimilate, implement, and recognize. The source of this misconception is the belief that marketing, sales, and service competencies are distinct competencies in marketing, sales, and service. In reality, most of the activities involved in the execution of marketing programs, sales initiatives, or customer service programs center around activities more closely related to a firm's customer information competency.

Information is their Business

One of the most important differences between masters and non-masters is the master's view that traditional business functional areas such as marketing, sales, and service are strategies to executive information competencies rather than distinct functions.

Activity	Information Master	Non-Information Master
Marketing	Executing customer information competency	Separate business function
Sales	Executing customer information competency	Separate business function
Customer Service	Required	Desired
Loyalty/Retention	An outcome	An initiative

For non-masters, information-related aspects of traditional functional business areas are only components of those areas. As a result, the firms are forced to spend more dollars in these areas to compensate for underlying weaknesses in their systemic information competencies.

A simple example is a leading US telecommunications provider who had made massive investments in technology for their customer database without investing in the communications between internal organizations. The result was many marketing campaigns that were replicated in different areas of the firm. One marketing campaign to several million customers was instituted as a direct mail campaign and at the same time was implemented as a coupon campaign to the same customer segment. As a result, the multi-million-dollar cost of one of the campaigns was a complete waste of company marketing resources.

Another example is one of the largest US mail-order retailers who had invested massive amounts in technology resources to understand the firm's customer transactions, without investing in the cross-origination link to measure advertising effectiveness. Their arch rival had invested more broadly in customer sales information with links to advertising effectiveness. In addition, their people were trained to watch for anomalies in sales activity. What they found was that every time their arch competitor ran a national ad campaign, their own sales experienced significant spikes. They were able to determine that their competitor had not sufficiently differentiated its product in the ad campaign; as a result, consumers were making calls to the competitor's 800 number to purchase gifts.

Rewards on the Road to Mastery

Firms reported that the rewards on the road to mastery far exceeded most investments in more traditional functional initiatives and infrastructure.

The reported bottom-line impacts could be categorized into two basic areas:

1   The value created from making better decisions.
2   The value created from making better decisions faster.

The value created from making better decisions was initially perceived as being the primary area of value. The speed impacts of improved customer information competency were frequently overlooked.

Closer analysis revealed that higher levels of customer information competency significantly increased the speed of a firm's proactive and reactive market actions. Analysis showed that the speed aspects of customer information competency accounted for roughly half of the entire benefit.

Speed of a Master

The speed at which firms are able to react to change and respond to the market as they developed their level of competency was clearly devastating to lesser-developed firms.

The impact of speed created two areas of value:

1   Proactive speed.
2   Reactive speed.

Proactive speed manifested itself in the ability to identify a market opportunity, enter it, and take a market segment before the competitors understood what had happened.

Reactive speed was exhibited by firms that would respond to a competitor's attack in predetermined ways almost instantaneously.

Although their ability to react increased as they moved along the continuum of customer information competency, the need for reactive speed decreased.

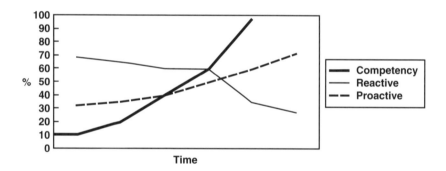

Figure 1.2   Proactive vs. reactive

Opportunity Reaction Time before Mastery

Before firms began to travel down the road to mastery, they would experience a tremendous lag in their ability to react to market opportunities because of an inability to gather, analyze, and apply the required information.

For example, one of the largest US investment brokers competed in a highly aggressive marketplace. In this example, they were anticipating changes in their market. Management felt that '. . . the

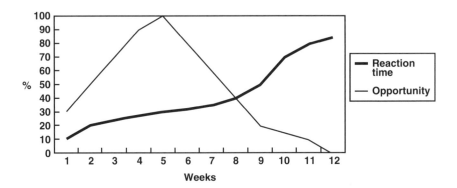

Figure 1.3   Before mastery – market reaction time

market is going to recuperate; certain product segments would do well; and we know certain customers would probably buy . . .'.

Having this market insight produced little benefit, because once the market was targeted it took two to four months to implement a marketing program because of their lack of ability to quickly apply the required market, customer, and operational information.

Their Senior VP explains, '. . . three months until we get our direct mail and marketing out'. By the time they complete all of their information gathering, analysis, and implementation, the campaign is no longer appropriate because market conditions have changed.

Reaction Time on the Road to Mastery

After firms had made more balanced investments in their information competency, their reaction times began to improve significantly.

Another leading US investment banking firm comments that now they could observe conditions in the marketplace change rapidly and move very quickly. They commented that they could develop very specific marketing lists in several days relative to economic conditions as an indicator of likely behavior.

They could now answer questions with great speed and accuracy within one week relative to:

✦   Who is likely to respond to this promotion?
✦   Which are my most valuable prospects?
✦   Which of my customers are most vulnerable to competitive offers?

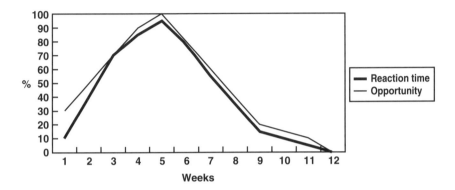

Figure 1.4   On the road to mastery – market reaction time

Reaction Time of an Information Master

At customer information mastery levels, 90% of the firm's resources are dedicated to proactive initiatives based on predictive capabilities. Their resources are centered on capturing business opportunities relative to consumer behavior, and then correlating that with economic conditions at the time.

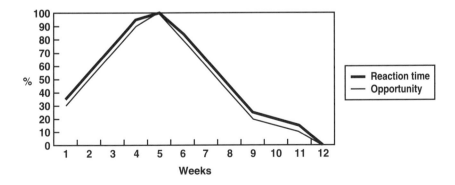

Figure 1.5   Information mastery – market reaction time

This is done with an advanced capability to:

+ Discover relationships
  — Many buying behaviors may not be immediately discernible and can significantly improve targeting.
+ Provide correct weights in statistical models
  — Income, geography and previous responsiveness have determined how much revenue can be generated by each customer
+ Simplify complexities of the business environment by advanced mathematics
  — Marketing to a segment-of-one is simplified by scoring each customer, i.e. using more information more accurately.

Competitive Attack Reaction Time

Opportunity reaction time before mastery

Before the firms started their journey on the road to mastery, they agreed that their reaction times to competitive attacks were either too slow, too uninformed, or both.

A leading US investment brokerage recounted a situation where their arch rival attacked one of their most profitable segments very late in the workweek hoping to get the jump on their best customers. After the firm realized what was occurring, they attempted to assess what the implications were for themselves as well as their customers. It took them two months to understand the financial implications of that attack. At this point, there were no formulated plans to counterattack, just an understanding of the financial implications. It took them another month to implement a counterattack, which they acknowledged was too little, too late. The figure below depicts the carnage.

Reaction Time on the Road to Mastery

As firms developed more information competency, they developed more speed.

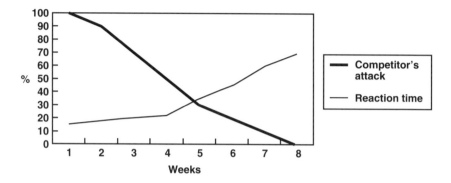

Figure 1.6   Before mastery – reaction to competitor's attack

A major US investment banking firm recounted that their ability to currently react to a competitor's attack was almost instantaneous, accurate,
and financially sound. This firm had the sophistication to pre-model
almost all likely scenarios that a competitor would employ. When the
competitors actually deployed one of these scenarios, they could
assemble an accurate and sound response within two business days.

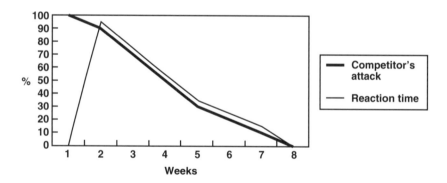

Figure 1.7   On the road to mastery – reaction time

Reaction Time of an Information Mastery

Again, the master predicts and therefore can be proactive.

This US investment banker's resources are focused not only on pre-
emptive strikes but also on creating real value for customers in order
to protect their best customers.

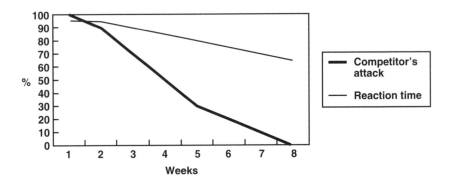

Figure 1.8   Information mastery – reaction time

Reaction Time to Sales Leads

This major US long-distance telecommunications firm had a significant challenge of applying information to sales opportunities in a timely fashion. Under the old information environment, when the information regarding new sales leads would finally be put into action, the business environment had changed and the leads were irrelevant.

Before this firm started on the road to mastery, it would take them an average of six weeks to respond to a sales lead with a volume of 90 million records per year. This was at a cost of $0.35 per lead.

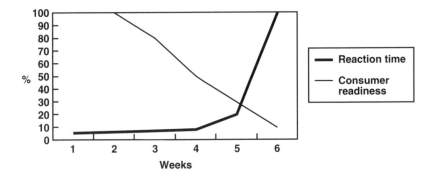

Figure 1.9   Before mastery – sales response time

On the Road to Mastery

As this telecommunications firm developed its information competency, it could respond to a lead in two hours with a volume of 150 million records per year. The cost of these leads dropped to $0.06 per lead. In 1997, the cost of leads went down to $0.04 per lead.

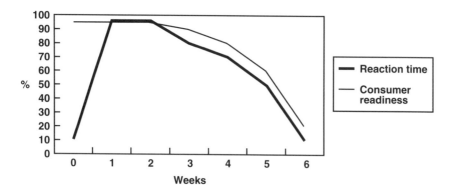

Figure 1.10   On the road to mastery – sales response time

Information Mastery Level – Sales Response Time

As this firm begins to approach information mastery, predicted response to leads will occur within the hour, with greater sales lead volumes. The cost of these leads is predicted to drop to $0.02 per lead.

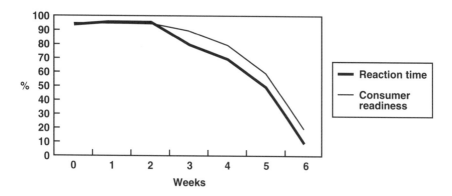

Figure 1.11   Information mastery – sales response time

Profitability and the Information Master

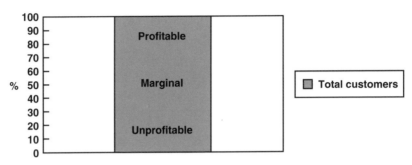

Figure 1.12   Profitability distribution

As firms progressed to higher levels of customer information competency, the relative awareness of profitability grew. Many firms were surprised to find just how narrow their band of profitable customers was, relative to their customer base.

Figure 1.12 represents a non-master's view of profitability. The view is an aggregate and offers little information for surgical initiatives.

Most firms agree that less than 20% of their current customers generate 80% or more of their total profitability. Many firms who have implemented activity-based costing as part of their information competency found that less than 5% of their customers represented the majority of their total profitability.

How well the firm understands its profitability can lead to new market opportunities. On the other hand, poor profitability measures can allow certain internal groups to cloak their poor business performance. One executive from a leading UK bank suggested that several groups within his organization developed great skill in hiding many poor financial and operational performances in their P&L because of the lack of detail and proper accountability.

Figure 1.13 shows a further evolution for a regional West Coast US bank on the road to mastery. The picture of profitability becomes clearer as well as the potential for decisive customer initiatives. From this detailed information, the firm can now target very specific customer segments for retention initiatives. They can also attempt to migrate these customers to higher levels of profitability.

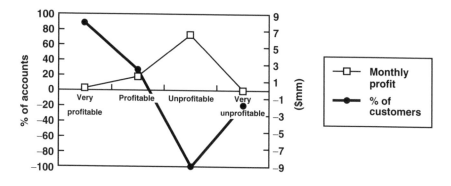

Figure 1.13   Percentage of customers vs. monthly profitability

Table 1.2 reveals a view closer to the mastery level with details revealing that only 0.019% of the customers were producing $3 021 332 out of $5 544 285 total profits. This small percentage of customers shows just how vulnerable and dependent firms are upon these customers.

Mastery and the Cost of Doing Business

Many firms before they start the journey to customer information mastery find themselves expending tremendous resources beyond what is

Table 1.2   Percentage profit per household

$ Profit/ Household	% of Household	% of Balance	$ Profit
Over $600	0.19%	2.34%	$3 021 332
$550 to 599	1.45%	1.53%	$945 321
$350 to 549	1.78%	4.22%	$1 353 798
$200 to 349	2.80%	9.35%	$4 354 323
$150 to 199	3.88%	7.55%	$3 456 387
$100 to 149	6.03%	31.87%	$2 435 678
$0 to 99	13.88%	12.44%	$978 453
−$1 to −25	22.34%	14.32%	−$7 345 234
−$26 to −49	33.78%	9.90%	−$2 435 654
−$50 to −74	13.64%	5.50%	−$877 954
Under −$75	0.23%	0.98%	−$324 165
Total	100.00%	100.00%	$5 544 285

necessary because of their underlying weakness in the information on which they are basing their initiatives.

One leading US investment banking firm would send out a tremendous volume of mailings to its customers in hopes that a very small percentage of them would respond. The basic criteria were that the customers have a certain number of products and that they transacted at least five times a year with the firm. The executives were aware that many of the mail campaigns were indiscriminate yet they did not have an alternative because of their inherent information weakness.

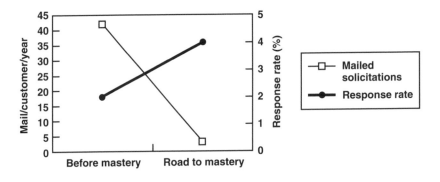

Figure 1.14   Reduction in mailings with increased response time

As the firm progressed down the road to mastery, it was able to radically reduce the number of mailings while at the same time doubling their response rate.

Mastery and Cross-Selling

Before beginning the road to mastery, many firms had the opportunity to cross-sell many products and services but lacked the information to do so. Even if they obtained the information, other missing elements of information competency such as cross-business-unit cooperation and incentives kept these very profitable initiatives from ever being launched.

One top UK bank found that when they had sufficiently developed information, cross-business-unit sharing, and leadership support, their ability to implement numerous and aggressive cross-selling initiatives skyrocketed. They also found that the added information perspectives from many business units caused the number of people who actually responded and purchased products to quadruple.

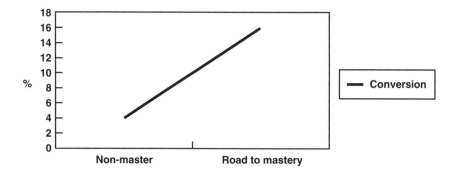

Figure 1.15   Mastery and cross sell

Mastery and Reducing Risk

Most firms did not have the customer information competency to accurately assess and then price for risk. Therefore, the firms typically under-priced the risky business and over-priced the less risky business. They also avoided very profitable business which may be inherently risky yet could be priced appropriately for the risk with the appropriate level of information competency.

One leading UK bank was avoiding writing certain loans because they couldn't price them accurately for the level of risk. After they began to develop their information competency, they were able to write higher-risk loans without increasing the percentage of loans that went bad.

One very aggressive US insurance company found itself avoiding the traditional high-risk segments of car insurance, which was consistent with the industry as a whole. As this firm developed its information competency, it was able to aggressively target a segment of high-risk insurance, which had been ostracized by its industry. It is now one of the largest sellers of car insurance in the industry with performance rates similar to companies insuring a lower-risk pool.

Mastery Marketing

Most of the firms in the research were able to obtain marketing response rates of 1–3%. Firms who had begun to lift their customer information competency were achieving consistent lifts of 5–7% above industry norms. Firms near mastery levels were able to consistently achieve 8–12% lifts above industry norms.

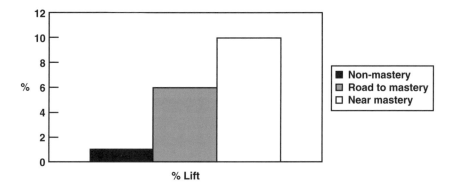

Figure 1.16   Evolution of marketing response rate lift

A Master's Customer Retention

For masters, retaining the right customers is an inherent byproduct of a deep understanding of customers and markets, not an isolated initiative.

This understanding and facility with customers came from a deep and broad customer information competency.

Firms report that as they traveled the road of mastery, they were able to steadily ratchet down their customer churn levels.

One large East Coast US bank depicted below found that they were able to reduce churn rates each year by at least one half of one percent relative to a current 6% churn rate. The firm did this by comparing economic cycles and customer behavior with appropriate product and services offerings. In doing so, they stopped a steady decline in good customers, while evolving moderately profitable customers into solidly profitable customers.

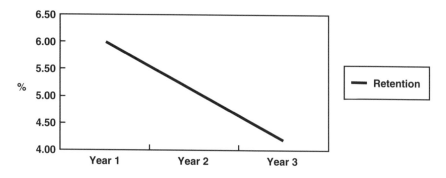

Figure 1.17   Evolution of retention

Mastery and Distribution Channel Effectiveness

Most firms, before they began their road to customer information competency, had distribution channels that operated with little knowledge of individual effectiveness and efficiency. In addition, as radical market changes caused radical changes in distribution channels, understanding the effect on customers was largely guesswork.

After developing further competencies, one leading Australian bank was able to reduce its channels by 20% and increase sales concurrently by 3%. This resulted from knowing the intimate interactions each customer had with each distribution channel and then fine-tuning these interactions to optimize value and profitability.

Mastery and Productivity

Most firms spend more of their productive time in information-related activities. When a firm can significantly reduce the time it takes to execute these activities, the firm can either:

1   Execute more business programs.
2   Execute the same business programs with less resources.

If the firm looks at how its time is spread between activities before the road to mastery, the mix is as in Figure 1.18.

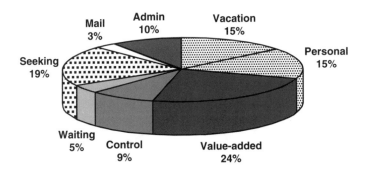

Figure 1.18   Typical working year (Source: PA Consulting Group)

As the figure depicts, 30% of employees' time is spent on vacation and personal time. The remaining 70% of employees' time is information-centric.

As firms evolved their competencies on the road to mastery, their productivity rose significantly because the amount of time spent in control, waiting, seeking, mail, and administration became less.

Business can be thought of as a series of decisions. If a firm can speed up decisions and the elements of making those decisions, productivity gains proliferate.

In addition, the time spent in value-added activities itself becomes more productive.

More advanced competency firms report productivity gains in some areas measuring ten times compared to lower competency levels.

One firm's allocation of time spent evolved to significantly higher value-added work time as Figure 1.19 depicts.

Masters Do More with Less

One of the most compelling but least talked about areas is the ability of firms to supplant workers with a near-mastery environment. It has long been thought that the age of automation was over. 'We have automated all the things we were able to with technology' is a belief often verbalized. 'We did that in the sixties and seventies.' In fact, information mastery gives us another level of automation. Firms have found

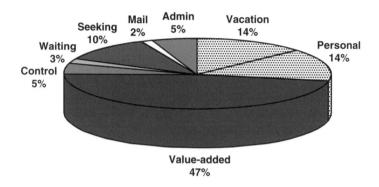

Figure 1.19   Typical working year – more advanced competency

that the employee time and resources required to find, extract, understand, and apply information for business in their current information environment is many times more than that in a near mastery firm.

'Faster, better, cheaper' can only be successfully applied when a firm is on the road to mastery. One firm found that after automation, most of their marketing workforce could have been re-deployed or reduced.

One leading US investment banking firm found that they could re-deploy roughly 45% of their corporate staff in marketing, sales, and service because the time required to complete activities was significantly reduced under higher information competency.

They went on to say that because of the firm's current culture, they could not actually reduce the workforce. They had never had to downsize and it was unheard of to do so. The mindset exhibited by this firm, like other firms, is changing quickly.

Many firms who have not had first-hand experience with the impacts on efficiency were skeptical of the tremendous productivity improvements. Disbelievers are quickly convinced once they see the operational changes a systemic information competency has on an employee's time spent in accomplishing tasks. The improvement flows from the employees whose jobs depend on information to accomplish their objective gives them more time for pure value-added work. Much of this improvement is in cycle time reduction.

Another impact of information competency on employee productivity is properly aligning the right level of information-related work with the right level of employee. As discussed earlier, information-related work is almost 90% of the employee's productive time.

Figure 1.20 depicts a director in a large US bank prior to transforming their information competencies. This director spent 25% of the time with information-related activities that were efficient for creating maximum added value for their position.

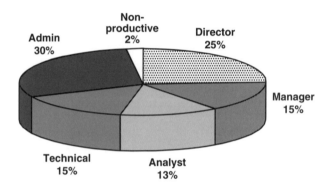

Figure 1.20   Director's level of information work

The director ends up doing lower-level work and not creating level-appropriate value or decisions. For example, the director spends time working with analyst-level information in order to make director-level decisions.

While from a cost-effectiveness perspective, the inefficiencies of information work at inappropriate levels quickly add up, the market opportunity costs from the director not operating at appropriate levels far exceeded the raw cost inefficiencies. Table 1.3 shows just the annual cost inefficiencies from director-level of this firm.

As this firm developed its information competency, there was a significant shift in level-appropriate work for information-related activities.

The annual cost saving was over one million dollars with estimated revenue opportunity cost savings estimated as three to five times that of cost savings.

Table 1.3 Annual cost inefficiencies from director level

Position	FTEs	Dir. Work	Mgr. Work	Anal. Work	Tech. Work	Admin. Work	Non-Prod. Work
Director	3	25%	15%	13%	15%	30%	2%
Manager	7	2%	32%	30%	10%	23%	3%
Analyst	12	0%	5%	37%	56%	1%	1%
Technical	8	0%	1%	2%	67%	28%	2%
Admin.	4	0%	0%	0%	0%	88%	12%
TOTAL	34						

Position	FTEs	Dir. Work	Mgr. Work	Anal. Work	Tech. Work	Admin. Work	Non-Prod. Work
Director	38	25%	15%	13%	15%	400%	2%
Salary level		$125 000	$95 000	$75 000	$65 000	$25 000	$125 000
Actual cost		$31 250	$18 750	$16 250	$18 750	$37 500	$2500
Cost level		$31 250	$14 250	$9750	$9750	$7500	$2500
Cost of time		$0	$4500	$6500	$9000	$30 000	$0
% of overpay		0%	32%	67%	92%	400%	0%
Cost of time × FTE		$0	$171 000	$247 000	$342 000	$1 140 000	$0
Cost inefficiency		$1 900 000					

Table 1.4 Annual cost efficiencies – on the road to mastery

Position	FTEs	Dir. Work	Mgr. Work	Anal. Work	Tech. Work	Admin. Work	Non-Prod. Work
Director	3	65%	10%	6%	9%	8%	2%
Manager	7	2%	32%	30%	10%	23%	3%
Analyst	12	0%	5%	37%	56%	1%	1%
Technical	8	0%	1%	2%	67%	28%	2%
Admin.	4	0%	0%	0%	0%	88%	12%
TOTAL	34						

Position	FTEs	Dir. Work	Mgr. Work	Anal. Work	Tech. Work	Admin. Work	Non-Prod. Work
Director	38	65%	10%	6%	9%	8%	2%
Salary level		$125 000	$95 000	$75 000	$65 000	$25 000	$125 000
Actual cost		$81 250	$12 500	$7500	$11 250	$10 000	$2500
Cost level		$81 250	$9250	$4500	$5850	$2000	$2500
Cost of time		$0	$3000	$3000	$5400	$8000	$0
% of overpay		0%	32%	67%	92%	400%	0%
Cost of time × FTE		$0	$114 000	$114 000	$205 200	$304 000	$0
Cost inefficiency		$737 200					

Information is the Master's Business

The most critical and distinguishing factor separating a true information master and a non-master is the fact that the firm has cognitively and culturally determined that regardless of their industry, product, or service, their business is information.

They understand that the success of a customer-focused business model is primarily dependent on their level of information competency. Therefore, they view business functions in the context of or as a subset of information competency.

Unless a firm has a relatively small number of customers and products, the mechanics of understanding customers and then making marketing, sales, and service decisions is accomplished through applying some form of previously acquired information. In smaller businesses, decisions can be made more spontaneously through business to customer contact without relying heavily on recorded information.

Information is the firm's primary view of the customer for marketing and sales decisions as well as for measuring and managing operational and financial performance. If this acquired information were removed, the firm would be blind, and in chaos. If the information existed but the ability to apply it were removed, similar conditions would result. This is becoming more the case as we move into an increasingly virtual business environment.

One major US retailer has been able to proactively and consistently lower prices through operational efficiencies. As a result, their non-master competitors have had to reactively lower prices through margin reduction.

The information master becomes stronger while the non-master becomes weaker.

Many firms are investing in traditional marketing areas to compensate for the lack of information competency. The same is true for sales and service initiatives. The results are quick but short-lived.

The masters are truly an anomaly in a world of mass-market information legacies.

By definition, details of this customer information obsession are
seldom published in the litany of trade and business journals. If
published, their stories are intentionally superficial.

Information masters view information competency as a primary
focus on:

1 Information competency as the core competency upon which all
   business functions rest.
2 Balancing investments in the elements of information competency, i.e. people, process, organization, culture, leadership,
   technology, and information itself.
3 Information as the organizational glue, not the boundaries.
4 Win–win value creation for both customers and shareholders.
5 Rewarding the value creation of information across organizations
   and initiatives.

The Non-Masters

Less developed competitors view information competency as a primary focus on:

1 Technological innovations such as corporate customer databases
   where data warehouses/marts/mining abound.
2 Information competency as the 'information' component, not a
   competency.
3 Marketing, sales, or service as an operational function rather
   than an information strategy for creating long-term value.

The emergence of the information masters as an information-based
competitor is here.

The secrets of the customer race lie in the ensuing information race.

The winners of the information race are the information masters
who have created a broad and deep ability to apply customer information in the context of customer and shareholder value.

To become a master, the answer lies in addressing the following issues in a balanced manner:

People

✦ Employ a balanced information mastery team.
✦ Include the following:
  — people with solid history of business operations;
  — people who are smart and very creative with minimal industry legacies;
  — people from IT who understand the business;
  — people from business who understand applying technology;
  — people who can sell the potential of the new environment;
  — people who have sophisticated math and statistical skills;
  — people who can apply more sophisticated and iterative information in customer contact environments.

Processes

✦ Change processes to optimize creation of value from the information.
✦ Optimize processes for the lower levels of information detail.
✦ Create information flows based on information value generation.
✦ Change existing processes to reflect new decision processes optimized for information detail.
✦ Remove processes which do not support new level of information detail.

Organization

✦ Establish clear reward systems for sharing information.
✦ Identify information hoarding groups and disarm them.
✦ Establish cross-function groups specifically dedicated to information innovation.

✦ Establish explicit budgeting of cross-business unit information sharing and modeling.

✦ Create a series of information products or services for each organization.

✦ Perform regular brainstorming sessions across business units.

✦ Aggressively educate business and IT on information value.

Culture

✦ Perform an information cultural audit to determine strengths and weaknesses.

✦ Determine the information cultural alignment between business and IT.

✦ Assess the cultural residue of mass-market information legacies.

✦ Assess people's belief of the importance of information in their jobs.

✦ Align customer culture levels with information culture levels.

✦ Identify and stop superficial cultural initiatives.

Leadership

✦ Identify leadership individuals who embrace the past and educate or remove them.

✦ Establish clear financial rewards for information transformation short and long term.

✦ Embed information directives across business functions.

✦ Identify a consistent chain of information visionaries at every management level.

✦ Do not attempt information transformation without a true information visionary.

Information

✦ Map phases of information aggregation and begin systematic desegregation.

✦ Identify where information is thrown away and examine potential value.

+ Assess percentage of known information available at point of contact and increase it.
+ Build a roadmap for evolving information quality and execute it.
+ Plan significant time to cross-match information sources.
+ Establish a roadmap for one informational 'truth'.

Technology

+ Retire legacy systems sooner than is perhaps comfortable.
+ Build an information environment which is efficient in both transaction and decision support.
+ Budget for the doubling of the primary information capabilities every two years.
+ Daily loads of all major systems.
+ Stop code develop on legacy systems.

2

Masquerade of a Hidden Malaise

ONE OF THE MOST CRITICAL ELEMENTS OF TRANSFORMING into a customer information master is seeing beyond the poor performance of traditional functions, seeing this not as a functional weakness but as a hidden sickness lying deep in the firm's underlying customer information proficiencies.

As discussed in the first chapter, firms invest major resources in high profile business initiatives such as sales, marketing, customer service, loyalty, retention, and profitability, only to find anemic rewards because of an underlying weakness in their firm's systemic ability to apply customer information. This weakness persists because firms address their competency to apply customer information as the information component of business functions rather than the foundation competency upon which all business functions exist. As a result, firms continue to invest a majority of their resources in the more comfortable and confined areas of enabling technologies, without addressing the crucial seven elements which determine the majority of the firm's information ability – people, process, organization, culture, leadership, and information itself.

The haze of traditional mass-market information legacies we've developed over the past fifty years cloaks this underlying weakness. Those who are responsible for the broad range of elements which determine the firm's information prowess, end up shielding the extent of the weakness because they are not empowered to change them.

Executives are particularly shielded from this malaise through unseen information heroics by subordinates who are responsible for delivering the unknowingly unrealizable information edicts.

Enter the information visionaries, a handful of visionary individuals who show up at the right place but the wrong time (twenty years too soon), who clearly recognize the ongoing corporate damage caused by this malady and, more importantly, feel a personal calling to attack this dysfunction against monumental odds.

This business dysfunction creates a host of corporate absurdities, which are now considered corporate norms.

Most firms:

✦ cannot accurately identify their exact number of customers;
✦ cannot accurately identify profit contributions by customer;
✦ engage in mass mail solicitations expecting a 97% failure rate;
✦ engage in personal phone contacts with little more than a name and address;
✦ cannot identify which promotions work on which customers;
✦ cannot identify their top customers across product groups;
✦ cannot tell whether a customer has been a customer previously;
✦ don't know what transpired during the last customer contact;
✦ cannot identify interrelationships between customers;
✦ apply less than 5% of their total information in making decisions;
✦ have a dangerously small 20% of customers generating 80% of its profit.

These absurdities are only a few embarrassing examples which firms privately acknowledge and publicly mitigate.

Occasionally, embarrassing evidence of the extent to which firms operate in the dark comes to public attention. In a recent mega-merger between to major firms, the sum of their separately claimed customer base totaled a number greater than the total of every man, woman and child in their country, an exercise in public mathematics they would have rather avoided. At the same time, both these firms are publicly regarded to be technologically advanced.

Other examples are known to only the inner circles of those who are involved. In one case, the US White House was considering closing many of the Air Force bases in California. The White House issued a request to all the major banks in this state for a quick assessment of total potential impact of closed bases and the effect the resulting job losses would have on each bank's current home loans, as well as the respective housing market. There were four major banks involved in this time-sensitive request. One of the four banks that had recognized their information malaise early on and had made significant progress responded to the White House in several weeks. The other banks simply could not answer the question.

Informational absurdities also take the form of legacy attitudes toward information. In one well-respected UK bank, one of the top executives is internally known for making the statement that:

> *'I have never let a lack of information interfere with my ability to make decisions.'*

. . . a statement which now haunts him as well as his firm.

These absurdities are generally excused as a given ineffectiveness rather than a soul-searching recognition of the failure to apply customer information properly.

The absurdities also manifest themselves in a lack of efficiency throughout the firm's operations. The speed at which the firm operates is primarily determined by the firm's efficiency in applying information. Again, this weakness is typically misconstrued as an ailment within the initiative rather than symptomatic of more profound information deficiency.

The following case study examples will explain typical manifestations of weak information competencies and how firms can link those surface weaknesses to the root cause of the systemic information weakness. In each of these case examples, the firm's focus was drawn to the surface problem, leaving the underlying problem unchecked. As a result, the firm's success in each business function was highly constrained. The case study examples used are three of the highest-profile business functions in a firm today:

✦   marketing and sales;
✦   loyalty and customer retention;
✦   profitability.

Marketing and Sales

The absurdity of marketing and sales today is that most initiatives are done without detailed information applied from other functions which have a direct bearing on a campaign's success, e.g. profitability, loyalty, and retention. Rather, most initiatives use very simple elements of profitability, retention, loyalty, and possible risk to calculate the propensity of a customer to accept a solicitation.

The reality is that predicting customer behavior and the resulting revenue value of that behavior requires very sophisticated information approaches beyond most firms' competency today.

When a marketing campaign is initiated, the consumer's behavior will be affected by a multitude of variables. Firms should use the following as a core set of variables in order to begin basic behavioral modeling. The answers to these questions are just the beginning:

+ At what point in time will the marketing campaign be executed?
+ What was the consumer's reaction to a similar previous campaign?
+ What was the consumer's reaction the day of the campaign?
+ What major life events will affect the campaign?
+ Which distribution channel will elicit the best response from the consumer?
+ Which distribution channel will produce the highest profitability?
+ Which marketing message will be optimized for which distribution channel?
+ Which campaign will optimize the reaction given a particular distribution channel?
+ How does predicted behavior and resulting profitability align with strategy?
+ How much should we pay for the campaign by individuals to create profitability?
+ How much should we pay for loyalty?

In a product-based environment with specific customers whose individual identity is obscured, a firm should use the following intertwined questions:

- ✦ Which product will a particular customer buy?
- ✦ What life event is linked to the product?
- ✦ Which store will sell the most to a particular individual?
- ✦ Which day is most conducive to selling a particular product to a particular person?
- ✦ What is the affinity between products purchased together for a particular person?

Add to this complexity a third dimension: accurately forecasting the consumer's buying behavior coupled with the issues of supplier forecasting for true collaborative forecasting and the information picture becomes extremely complex.

On the surface: marketing response problem

A firm's ability to effectively respond to a market is inextricably linked to a firm's systemic information ability, yet remedies are continuously misdirected to the symptoms rather than the root cause. This example illustrates that linkage and the resulting low performance of their marketing department's ability to respond to a fast and complex marketplace with low information competency.

In the example in the first chapter, one firm competed in a highly aggressive marketplace. In this example, they were anticipating changes in their market. Their management felt that '. . . the market is going to recuperate; certain product segments would do well; and we know certain customers would probably buy . . .'.

This was clearly not a lacking in marketing strategy or competence but the availability of customer and market information.

On the surface: competitive response problem

A firm's ability to effectively respond to a competitor is also inextricably linked to a firm's systemic information ability. Many firms still remedy the symptoms rather than the underlying cause. This example illustrates that linkage and the resulting low performance of their market function's ability to respond to a fast and aggressive competitor under low information competency.

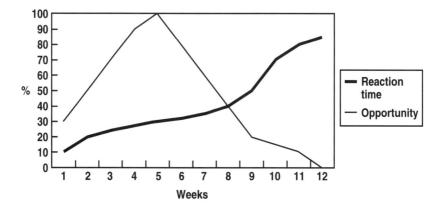

Figure 2.1   Before mastery – market reaction time

As described in the first chapter, the US investment bank attempts to respond in a timely fashion to an arch rival attacking one of their most profitable segments very late in the workweek. As they find out, the information which they require to make an accurate assessment of damage to their customer base and potential future business is locked up in multiple information fortresses.

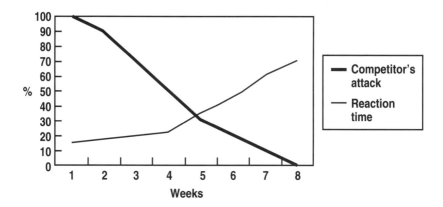

Figure 2.2   Before mastery – reaction to competitor's attack

This has little to do with their traditional competencies as marketing strategists but more to do with their raw ability to access sales, marketing, and customer profitability information in short order.

On the surface: high customer solicitation costs

A firm's ability to accurately target customers in a given market is a direct function of the firm's systemic information ability, yet attentions continue to be directed toward reducing soaring marketing campaign costs rather than the lack of information competency which created the inefficiencies. There are high marketing costs for a firm whose approach relies heavily on mailed solicitations as a primary vehicle. Most firms spend tremendous amounts of capital on mailed solicitation campaigns for prospective customers. As discussed earlier, current corporate norms suggest that 97% of these mailings ended up in the garbage can. So 97% of the *cost* of the solicitation has no hope of ever being recovered.

One US investment brokerage was known for its very aggressive marketing activities, but their efforts were a fisherman casting a large net in an attempt to catch a particular type of fish without any knowledge of the habitat and behavior of the fish. As a result, their prospective customers were inundated with solicitations despite the fact there was little possibility of them responding to the firm's products and services. The vast amounts of mail that were sent to unqualified groups of customers were also becoming a great source of irritation to recipients.

Statistically, if a current customer carried four products and performed at least one transaction per year, the firm would send out one hundred and sixty solicitation offers. In hindsight, their top marketing VP regarded many of their solicitations as:

> *'Very foolish direct mail campaigns.'*

This visionary comments on the ROI:

> *'. . . We invested $4 million, and made it back on mailing costs in the first year.'*

On the surface: sales lead response problem

As discussed in the first chapter, a particular telecommunications firm had a significant problem pursuing sales opportunities to capitalize on market opportunities in sync with the marketplace.

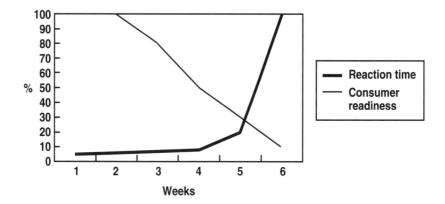

Figure 2.3   Before mastery – sales response time

Their inability to react in the old information environment was not a weakness in sales management, their sales force, or sales support, but a weakness in their ability to collect and describe information on sales leads.

Loyalty and Retention

Loyalty programs today address customer retention without detailed information as to the price of that loyalty. Business typically does not know the specific value of keeping a customer, just that they want to develop overall loyalty.

What about loyalty schemes? They are just that – schemes based on a scheme, not on value. They are pervasive in the industry, and fairly effective in drawing people to participate in the scheme. Unfortunately, that's where the behavior typically ends. If the firm carefully examines the behavior or loyalty generated by the scheme, they will find loyalty, not to the firm, but to the scheme itself.

On the surface: loyalty schemes create loyalty

Loyalty can only be achieved through a clear understanding of a customer. This understanding is represented by detailed information and the ability to operationalize this information. This ability can only be achieved through a sophisticated information competency. Sustaining this loyalty is done through an iterative flow of evolving customer information in a simple manner.

Most loyalty schemes create loyalty only to the scheme because they are executed with superficial understandings of customer needs and behavior relative to product or service utility. As a company gets progressively more competitive and reactive to competitors, the absurdities escalate. This escalation was rampant in UK food retailers. It started when one retailer announced their loyalty card could only be redeemed in their stores. As competition stiffened, they announced that their competitor's Card B could be redeemable in their stores as well. As a reaction, Retailer B announced that their card could now be redeemed in Retailer B's stores. Retailer A then announced that shoppers could redeem double points from their Card A. Retailer B then announced that it would honor double points in their store for Retailer A's card. One particular customer of Retailer A redeemed £1000 of credit from Retailer B's coupons. Thus, loyalty grew for the cards, but not the retailers.

The only way to truly understand and earn loyalty is by understanding your customer needs and behavior. The only way to do this is through analyzing and predicting needs and behavior with sophisticated information techniques.

In essence, schemes not soundly based on information are just baby dinosaurs waiting to hatch.

Recent corporate history is overflowing with legendary loyalty schemes, which failed because they did not utilize sufficient information to predict behavior and resulting cost and benefits to both customers and shareholders.

On the surface: the right price for loyalty

To effectively determine and manage the price of loyalty, a firm must model sophisticated and complex customer relationships, their financial attributes, with information. Most remedies for pricing loyalty are targeted at relative market norms rather than a price which is appropriate for the individual firm. The resulting loyalty pricing miscalculations create strategy and marketing havoc in the firm.

CITIBANK and Ford Motor attempted a major joint initiative based on rebates from a joint credit card but underestimated the negative impact the rebate would have on both firms. The co-branded card offered a 5% rebate on every purchase made with the card. Ultimately, CITIBANK and Ford Motor ended up canceling the co-branded card because the cost far outweighed the benefits to shareholders.

Another well-known example was a US telecommunications firm's entry into the credit card business. Their main loyalty scheme was to offer customers credit cards with no annual fee for life. They built a tremendously large customer base in a very short time. By their measurements, they were performing quite well. Ultimately, because the fee scheme didn't accurately predict consumer behavior and its resulting cost and benefits, almost 60% of the cardholders were inactive. In other words, 60% of their cardholders generated no fee income or late charges but created enormous relative administrative and processing costs. To put this in perspective, this firm had 18 million cardholders representing $14 billion in business 'convenience cardholders'.

Information mastery is the key to improving the credit-card industry's current level of cardholders deemed undesirable (30–40%).

Another good example is GE, who entered into the fray with a Rewards MasterCard. This card had no annual fee and paid customers rewards based on annual purchases made on the card. Under this program, a majority of their cardholders did not 'revolve' their payments, which meant no interest was incurred. GE eventually had to institute a new $25 annual penalty because of insufficient interest-bearing debt from customers. Again, information mastery is the key to improving the ability to predict customer behavior from incentives.

On the surface: losing customers . . . but who?

A firm's ability to understand and manage the ebb tide of customers is continuously misdirected at the absolute numbers rather than the attributes of the numbers, resulting in blind management of customer flows in a complex marketplace under low information competency. Firms are very concerned about losing customers. As a matter of course, they spend great resources to retain customers, but most of these efforts don't detail the desirability of individual customers. Most firms still struggle with the definition of a customer.

One set of competing firms who participated in the research conveyed a perfect mirror story reflecting their specific competitive environment. One well-established firm states that they were losing fifteen hundred customers a month to this very aggressive start-up firm in their market. When asked what type of customers they were losing – very profitable ones? long-term customers? – they did not know the answer.

The firm who was plundering these customers participated in the same research and conveyed the same story but from the opposite perspective. This very aggressive call-center-based UK start-up shared the fact that they were poaching fifteen hundred customers a month from this more staid firm. When questioned whether they had modeled the desirability of these customers they had plundered, they unequivocally responded, 'yes'. They had modeled these customers in a very sophisticated attribute matrix and were simply plundering only the most profitable.

Profitability

As ridiculous as it may sound, most firms execute only very crude profitability measures in customer relationship initiatives.

Understanding profitability well necessitates that a firm very accurately represents and allocates costs and revenues. Many firms will publicly suggest they in fact do have this area well in order but privately admit they are quite primitive.

Profitability is very complex as a field of study, covering cost allocation, transfer pricing, profitability over time, predictors of profitability, and cross-business unit profitability. But complexity itself is really not the limiting factor so much as applying complex information in an operationally effective and efficient way.

As most firms have neither the information rigor of profitability measurement nor the environment in which to apply it effectively, making decisions about customers and operations is compromised. Even for those firms that have managed to develop reasonably rigorous measurements, proactive business decisions are still quite a distant reality.

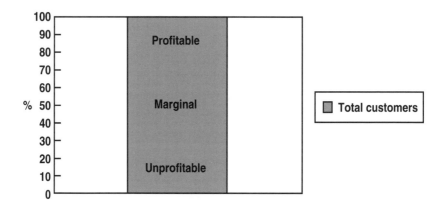

Figure 2.4   Profitability distribution

This shortfall is evidenced by the profitability composition of most firms' customer bases. In the firms studied who have started to measure basic profitability, the highest percentage of customers determined to be profitable was 25%. The lowest was 2%. The average percentage of profitable customers was roughly 15%.

On the surface: aggregate profitability

The effective response to a market is inextricably linked to systemic information ability. One US bank's profitability picture shows how vulnerable a firm can be.

As discussed in the first chapter, this US long-distance telecommunications firm reveals that only 0.019% of the customers were producing $3 021 332 out of $5 544 285 total profits. This small percentage of customers shows just how thin a firm's existence really is.

Would a firm consciously choose to run a business in which only 0.19% of its customers contributes to profits? No. The explanation is simple – the firms do not have sufficient information or the ability to apply it proactively to avoid losing their best customers, or continuing to service the unprofitable ones.

Ironically, as firms progressed in measuring and allocating profitability, they learned that the actual percentage number of profitable customers previously thought profitable becomes smaller.

Table 2.1   Percentage profit per household

$ Profit/ Household	% of Household	% of Balance	$ Profit
Over $600	0.19%	2.34%	$3 021 332
$550 to 599	1.45%	1.53%	$945 321
$350 to 549	1.78%	4.22%	$1 353 798
$200 to 349	2.80%	9.35%	$4 354 323
$150 to 199	3.88%	7.55%	$3 456 387
$100 to 149	6.03%	31.87%	$2 435 678
$0 to 99	13.88%	12.44%	$978 453
–$1 to –25	22.34%	14.32%	–$7 345 234
–$26 to –49	33.78%	9.90%	–$2 435 654
–$50 to –74	13.64%	5.50%	–$877 954
Under –$75	0.23%	0.98%	–$324 165
Total	100.00%	100.00%	$5 544 285

Only 0.19% of most firms' total customers keeps them in business. This concept is very unsettling at board levels and tends to be met with denial. Yet those who support the firm's information development and application for profitability privately are aware of the lack of detail in this area.

On the surface: inactive customers

One leading UK bank decided to do some basic profitability assessments on their customer base. They subsequently found that a small percentage were extremely unprofitable, and decided to jettison them in hopes of not only losing them but inviting them to visit their competitors instead. They created a campaign to write a nice thank-you letter accompanied with a check to close their current account balance. This seemed to be the right approach at the time, but results of the mailing were quite unexpected. They found that many in this unprofitable segment were actually deceased. As a result, many of the checks were never cashed.

3

Mass-Market Customer Information Legacy

M OST FIRMS' DEEPLY ENTRENCHED LEGACY OF APPLYING customer information to mass markets is underestimated in scope, underrated in its consequence, unrelenting in its resolve, and unmitigated in its quiet power to destroy well-intentioned customer initiatives. It is also the source of one of the most dominant fallacies of today's business environment – the misbelief that we are currently in the information age. The customer information legacy permeates deep into the consciousness of every firm in business today. Ultimately, it is our ball and chain to the 20th century.

We are not in an information age but in an age of information. The information age existed one hundred years ago, without technology, in a simpler world. The world today is complex and filled with massive amounts of information, without the competency to use it. We seek to return to an age of customer intimacy with its natural customer information competencies of fifty years ago.

Our mass-market information legacy has been in the making for half a century. It came to be through the slow evolution of businesses making large-scale efforts to service large-scale markets. The legacy functioned well in those markets, but is dysfunctional today as businesses seek once more to service markets intimately.

One US investment banking executive captures the essence of decisions in the mass-market information legacy:

> '. . . Business decisions in my firm are driven by internal power battles with customers as the secondary influence.'

This environment is in contrast to one where decisions are made based on the merit of actual facts which are available at any level to support predictive and iterative decision-making.

Information Anemia

Many firms have realized they were conducting business with surprisingly little customer information. Consistently, important business decisions concerning customers and operations were being made on surprisingly few facts relative to all the unknowns in a given business decision. A large part of the mass-marketing information legacy is a focus on what firms already know, not what they need to know.

Many customer approaches have been biased towards capturing customer information to limit the potential downside of a customer relationship instead of proactively soliciting information to enable them to address the upside. Add to this all of the information locked in paper, file cabinets, branches, organizations, and countries, and the abyss of unknowns in which decision-makers operate emerges.

One major US investment banking executive commented that his firm's people in the field deal with their customers without access to truly useful information:

> '. . . Our field organizations operate in an abyss.'

He went on to say:

> '. . . The field doesn't have the customer information it needs to gain that extra competitive edge as well as lacking the information it needs to service the customer after the sale.'

Neither did they have the information to determine the actual performance of their operations.

Many firms came to the realization that an information-oriented environment would provide the detail necessary to implement measurement programs such as activity-based costing. Others worried that this type of detailed information would reveal the operational sins hidden in the aggregated data. In many cases the firms developed initiatives without really knowing the true effect on the individual firm's performance. As one UK banking executive eloquently illustrates:

> '*Our firm is not sure our destination is preferable to the place we started from.*'

It is not just the intrinsic value of the customer information but the speed with which it can be applied. Most firms described their information infrastructure as extremely slow. The speed and ability of the firm to respond is graphically drawn by one US investment banking executive:

> '*After we figure out all the questions we need to ask about our market and customers, record them, request an answer, get an answer, the market and customers are different.*'

The lack of speed has two costs.

1 The firm gives up revenue opportunities because it knows it cannot address them before their competitor does.
2 The lack of timely information causes a delayed response to changing market conditions and thus causes the firm to focus on outdated market conditions.

Certain highly regulated industries such as banking and insurance that have been informationally weak have developed decision-making shortcuts. While this has worked in the past, the dynamics of a consumer-intensive industry has antiquated these shortcuts, and in fact made them increasingly dangerous.

Given the critical decisions made by simple rules of thumb and the consequences of poor decisions, it is incredible that decision-makers still utilize these methods.

The mass-market customer information legacy includes all facets of the business:

- ✦ the people, who collect, store, analyze, and apply customer information;
- ✦ the processes through which the customer information is applied;
- ✦ the organizational structures through which customer information is given specific purpose and form;
- ✦ the leadership from which comes customer information, direction, and control;
- ✦ The information culture, a collection of beliefs as to the proper use and value of customer information;
- ✦ the information technology that determines the form and function of customer information;
- ✦ the customer information itself.

This information legacy gives businesses massive amounts of information, but not the right information. Businesses have information overload yet not enough information. Businesses profess that they are drowning in customer information, not better customer information.

The Real Information Age

To begin charting a course for future customer information competency, a firm must fully understand the forces that drive information-based competition. It is appropriate to first examine the evolution (or de-evolution) of a firm's use of information (knowledge) over the past hundred years. One hundred years ago the mechanics of business were very similar to today's. The principles of customer focus have not changed over time, but the processes and methods employed by firms have.

How did the corner grocer of yesteryear use information to make profitable decisions in the market? These grocers operated in a much less complex community where business people interacted with customers at a far more personal level. When making a decision, proprietors drew upon a multifaceted knowledge base. Often, they had a personal relationship with the customer, perhaps even knew the customer's sons and daughters. The customer and grocer many times intermingled on a personal level outside the context of the firm. They may have attended the same place of worship. They may have had a similar group of friends. Their wives may have been friends, attending the same social functions. Having this multifaceted interaction meant that the corner grocer knew such details as personality or preferences. The grocer had a sense of the customer from past interactions or discussions with local shop owners that revealed whether a future customer was likely to repay and when.

Overall, there were fewer competitors, fewer customers, and fewer products – in other words, less complexity. With business on a smaller scale, there was less information to apply. Business transactions more closely resembled interactions between friends rather than today – dealings with a firm's massive infrastructure.

In addition, points of contact were generally face to face. Proprietors typically managed businesses on a smaller scale and therefore could retain almost every aspect of the financial and operational details in their heads. Employees interacted with customers both personally and professionally. The distinction between the two worlds was often blurred. Businesses were naturally intertwined with the lives of their customers. As such, the richness of information held in the head of proprietor and employee alike eclipsed that of today's relative business knowledge, and existed naturally without a single microchip.

Beyond the human ability to retain this relatively detailed knowledge of their business, they also had the natural ability to apply it efficiently and effectively. Simply, they had a natural appreciation for the value of information. Elements of complex corporate structures didn't exist. Consequently, the pace of business and decision-making was significantly faster than today. Back then, decision-makers had the right information without organizational complexity and dizzying decision processes. Most importantly, their information culture applied information naturally. After all, business is simply a series of decisions.

As business evolved, people failed to keep pace with developing new information skills required to apply stored information effectively in complex business environments. Business processes evolved into complex ritual, which stagnated decision-making.

Organizations had grown immense, each business unit building its own information fortress. The evolved information culture was focused on efficient processes while minimizing the cost of 'dealing' with the firm's information. The appreciation of and ability to naturally create value from information was now a corporate relic. At the same time, corporate culture evolved from one of community and friendship to one of politics and process.

As our world and its businesses grew in complexity, information about business grew beyond a human's ability to remember and apply it effectively. Information began its migration to record-keeping tools such as paper and ledgers. Paper and ledgers gave way to mechanical devices. Mechanical devices gave way to early forms of vacuum tube and transistorized computers. During this process, the amount of overall information grew in scale and complexity while the rich detail of information about customers and operations decreased.

As information migrated from inside to outside human minds, businesses became more detached from the realities of their business environments. As workers became more detached from their information, they became more detached from their customers, their operations, and the financial realities of their businesses.

During this time, technology progressed in its ability to store and process transactional information. This was falsely consoling to business because technology's role, to actually support decision making rather than just process data, had not yet entered the mainstream of corporate thinking. Businesses were often intoxicated by technology's ability to process vast amounts of transaction-related data. Simultaneously with the evolution of technology, businesses grew more complacent about the details of customers and operations. Complacency went unnoticed because their competitors were experiencing the same numbness.

Technology design during this period aided the processing of transactions, not better decision making and making better decisions faster. While this era was heralded as the heyday for mainframe computers, their early design limitations forced businesses to continue aggregating and summarizing customer and operational details.

As stated earlier, the summarization of information produced further customer detachment. The customer's detachment produced a culture. The culture became a corporate tradition. Both firms and customers progressively became unfeeling to this emerging culture of remoteness and indifference.

This trend was gradual and for the most part unnoticed because most firms drifted in information currents. The rate of this information aggregation was driven not only by technology limitations but also by the growing complexity of the modern market.

The days when a proprietor acquired visual cues such as quality of dress and even current emotional state or mood of the customer were fading. The proprietor's intimate knowledge of the local market was replaced by broader, aggregate views. The proprietor's awareness of local economic cycles which determined the financial wellbeing of the customer's business, and thus their personal buying power, was replaced by general business trends.

The business transactions of one hundred years ago had characteristics more closely related to those of a friendship or personal relationship than a strict business transaction. From this relationship orientation, the businessperson could make a better risk/reward decision and at the same time the customer felt genuinely more satisfied. The relative amount of information that a proprietor used to make a good decision far exceeded the amount of information used today. It is arguable that the businessperson of one hundred years ago made better business decisions without massive computer systems. The anatomy and logic of relationship-oriented transactions seem eloquently simple and beneficial for both the businessperson and customer.

How have firms drifted so far from this information-rich, relationship-oriented environment? The answer is simple: the world became more complex. As the community grew, the number of customers grew. As the customer base grew, the firms grew in size and number of locations. So did the number of competing firms. As customers' needs diversified, firms expanded the number of products and services. All of this brought added complexity to the visionary's world. Firms reacted to this added complexity in a seemingly logical manner. They began aggregating and summarizing their customer and operational information. This aggregation and summarization happened gradually, matching the growing level of complexity in the marketplace.

Both proprietor and customer gradually became numb to this growing culture of distance. The interaction between proprietor and customer grew into what today is a typical business interaction, an exchange between the customer and firm that is impersonal and unsatisfying.

Why have firms sunk to such a low customer service level?

Simply put, because they could.

Why have customers permitted corporations to deal with them so callously?

Simply put, because they didn't have a good choice.

Even if businesses had wanted to become more intimate with their customers, they did not have the proficiency to record and treat the mass of very detailed information. Firms only talked about these information proficiencies and customers had no choice but to wait for better services. These services could not be delivered because relationship-oriented service requires a precise understanding of customers and logistics, which requires massive volumes of information that must be accessible and usable. The firms' current 'information' technology infrastructure kept that very information locked up in information fortresses.

In the last twenty years, as firms have looked for ways to differentiate themselves from competitors, two market forces converged. There was a growing appreciation that customer satisfaction could produce competitive advantages. Many firms raised the customer-focus banners and declared that they were a customer-focused, relationship-oriented business. For most firms, this turned out to be a hollow threat, consisting mainly of internal binders and mottoes proclaiming magical customer experiences. To a large extent, these schemes failed because of a lack of commitment and of the true realization of what it takes to create it. In most cases, it wasn't a lack of available information but the insufficient capacity to process the complexities of the information and then apply it efficiently and effectively to customers' needs and shareholders' goals alike.

The real 'information age' existed one hundred years ago when business was conducted between proprietor and customer. The proprietor knew each customer personally. The proprietor also knew the logistical nuances of each product and operational details of every service. Intertwined with this rich information was the detailed awareness of the relative financial contributions of each customer, product, and service. This information-rich environment was possible because the proprietor was one individual who operated in a small market.

All aspects of the business's information resided in the head of the proprietor. As such, the information retention and processing occurred naturally, bounded only by intellectual capacity. Applying information to customer-oriented decision-making in this manner occurred instantaneously.

Information Environment	19th Century Proprietorship
Competitor market approach	Segment of one
Actual information ability	Atomic, iterative, predictive
Market complexity	Simple
Market scope	Local
Information horizon	Lifetime of business
Customer information	Full sensory, natural
Operational information	Detailed, intimate
Financial information	Detailed, intimate
Business relationship to information	Experiential, personal
Nature of information	Visual, auditory, behavioral
Skills optimization	Full sensory, natural
Process optimization	By customer and product
Organization optimization	Segment of one
Technology optimization	None
Collection points	Mind of proprietor
Storage points	Mind of proprietor and paper
Processing tool	Mind of proprietor
Speed of decision-making	Instantaneous
Number of information layers	One

As businesses grew in scale and complexity (more customers, products, and services), the proprietors began relinquishing the intimate connection they had with their business and its customer information.

First, business's increasing information volume and complexity grew beyond the proprietor's intellectual abilities to accurately recall and apply it. Out of necessity, the proprietor began recording more basic transaction details externally, e.g. paper, mechanical accounting machines. This recorded information was only a summarization of the basic business transaction relative to the proprietor's total information surrounding the transaction.

As business continued to grow, the addition of employees fragmented the once central point of information collection and storage of the proprietor. As business grew further, added management functions stratified levels of customer information collection and storage.

The gradual separation of the proprietor from the once hands-on, intimately detailed approach came from increased scale and information complexity. These changes to the 19th century proprietor's business would be a harbinger to greater customer information detachment and summarization during the mass-market approaches of the 20th century.

Information Environment	19th Century Proprietorship	20th Century Corporation
Competitor market approach	Segment of one	Mass market
Actual information ability	Atomic, iterative, predictive	Aggregated mass market
Market complexity	Simple	Complex
Market scope	Local	Regional
Information horizon	Lifetime of business	1–5 years
Customer information	Full sensory, natural	Aggregated, static, administrative
Operational information	Detailed, intimate	Aggregated, static, administrative
Financial information	Detailed, intimate	Aggregated, static, administrative
Business relationship to information	Experiential, personal	Aggregated, static, administrative
Nature of information	Visual, auditory, behavioral	Static reporting and measurement
Skills optimization	Full sensory, natural	Aggregated, administrative
Process optimization	By customer and product	Aggregated product and customer
Organization optimization	Segment of one	By masses in aggregate
Technology optimization	None	Summarized transactional
Collection points	Mind of proprietor	Employees and machines
Storage points	Mind of proprietor and paper	Multiple technology platforms, paper
Processing tool	Mind of proprietor	Multiple technology platforms
Speed of decision-making	Instantaneous	Weeks to months

Business's ability to apply the same relative detail in a larger market was no longer possible and therefore the application of information evolved toward mass information for the developing mass market. Not only did the use of information become more aggregated, it shifted from a central role to a supportive role focusing on internal measurement and control. The slow evolution of information tools perpetuated this mass approach. Thus, information began its relative descent of perceived importance and value.

Every aspect of business's corresponding operations and infrastructure aligned to support this same information approach for larger markets. The people, processes, organizations, and the supporting technology were optimized for the mass application of information. People's information skills were developed and rewarded for applying information in the aggregate within their fragmented view of the business. Processes were optimized for summarized transactional information, which were efficient given the market size. The growth in business size resulted in the growth of organizational structures producing greater information fragmentation and segregation.

In this last half-century, the evolution and design of business technology (ironically named 'information' technology) and its support infrastructure formed to apply information to mass markets.

In the mid-80s, a promising technology emerged in the market that was capable of processing massive amounts of information that greatly exceeded the processing capabilities of the firms' largest mainframes. This new technology, referred to as 'decision support' or 'massively parallel processing', gave firms the potential to process the vast amounts of information necessary to truly become customer-focused. This new information processing capability would also allow them to better understand and manage the operational dynamics and balance the intricacies of risk and reward in the business.

The firms were slow to adopt these 'information machines' in large part because of the perceived 'radical' nature of this technology. The firms' technological environment had been dominated for decades by the classic mainframe with limited information-processing capabilities. The early mainframes couldn't provide the firms with the level of detailed information they needed to really understand their business beyond an aggregated view, but were both a reliable and a 'known' technology. Although several progressive firms began investing in the new 'information machines', this type of technology was still considered higher risk relative to traditional transaction-processing technologies. As these progressive firms learned, they began to understand the power of information, started to see positive results, and increased their investment in information initiatives. The early adapters were finding ROIs atypically high relative to returns from other technology investments, and were achieving a tremendous competitive advantage. Thus began the wave of information-based competition. Other firms quickly followed out of fear.

Although these information machines were beginning to be acquired, the approach was still viewed as 'lunatic fringe' relative to the tried and true mass-market optimized mainframe technology.

Coinciding with these new technology developments was an increased awareness that business has grown desperately out of touch with the fine details of its customers and self. This awareness fueled much of the rapid growth in the management consulting industry as firms attempted to depart from the mass-market approach. Much of their efforts focused on the symptoms of mass-market legacy, not the underlying drivers that created the market approach. These symptoms span the gamut of business malady, e.g. poor customer service, fleeting loyalty, ineffective marketing, mediocre financial management, and inefficient operations and logistics.

Business used mass-market approaches because they couldn't apply information to the rich extent to which they had applied it on a smaller scale. This deep information legacy, which evolved over half a century, has crystallized attitudes, operations, and infrastructure surrounding information for markets in the aggregate.

The Crossroads – 20th Century Competency and 21st Century Imperatives

We are at the market juncture of 20th century mass-markets and 21st century segment-of-one markets. The desire of firms to achieve success with these 21st century business imperatives are kept at bay by their 20th century customer information proficiencies.

Information Environment	19th Century Proprietorship	20th Century Corporation	Market Transition Phase
Competitor market approach	Segment of one	Mass market	Segment of one
Actual information ability	Atomic, iterative, predictive	Aggregated mass market	Aggregated mass market
Market complexity	Simple	Complex	Very complex
Market scope	Local	Regional	Global
Information horizon	Lifetime of business	1–5 years	1–5 years
Customer information	Full sensory, natural	Aggregated, static, administrative	Aggregated, static, administrative
Operational information	Detailed, intimate	Aggregated, static, administrative	Aggregated, static, administrative
Financial information	Detailed, intimate	Aggregated, static, administrative	Aggregated, static, administrative
Business relationship to info	Experiential, personal	Aggregated, static, administrative	Aggregated, static, administrative
Nature of information	Visual, auditory, behavioral	Static reporting and measure	Static reporting and measure
Skills optimization	Full sensory, natural	Aggregated, administrative	Aggregated, administrative
Process optimization	By customer and product	Aggregated product and customer	Aggregated product and customer
Organization optimization	Segment of one	By masses in aggregate	By masses in aggregate
Technology optimization	None	Summarized transactional	Summarized transactional
Collection points	Mind of proprietor	Employees and machines	Employees and machines
Storage points	Mind of proprietor and paper	Multiple technology platforms, paper	Multiple technology platforms, paper
Processing tool	Mind of proprietor	Multiple technology platforms	Multiple technology platforms
Speed of decision-making	Instantaneous	Weeks to months	Weeks to months

New business imperatives demand very complex customer information environments, which dwarf the environment of the mass market. The globalization of many firms has added an increasingly diverse set of information proficiencies. The predictive abilities needed in the new markets are extremely difficult given the one- to five-year useable information horizon applied by most firms. The firms are striving for atomic approaches to markets yet the information is still predominantly summarized. Many firms have physically deployed the beginning of 21st century information machines, yet not invested in the other information competency.

A Legacy with Great Resolve

There are many reasons for the steadfastness of this legacy. Firstly, the ability to apply customer information is simply overlooked as a distinct core competency.

Another reason for the resolve of this legacy is that many firms believe that they have higher information competency than their actual abilities. The most advanced firms placed their relative information competency extremely low relative to the future potential growth in this competency. The handful of extremely informationally advanced firms placed their information competency very low on a scale reflecting their potential ability to apply information in the future. Most firms, while having relatively low information competency, placed themselves relatively high on the information competency scale.

The most advanced firms start out with a lower perception of their abilities. This creates added impetus for growth.

As a result, the very advanced firms felt a deep compulsion to drive even harder to higher levels of information competency.

In contrast, the majority of the firms start with a higher self-perception of their information competency. This creates complacency and slow progression.

The effective use of a firm's information exists only in small pockets. This results primarily from the absence of a deep appreciation of the role information plays in the firm's success or decline.

As a result, customer information initiatives continue to be categorized as technology initiatives. In most cases, the existence of data

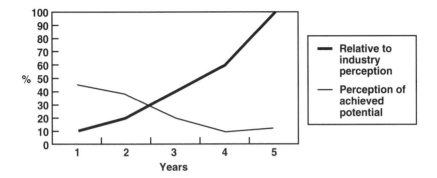

Figure 3.1 Information competency – most advanced firms

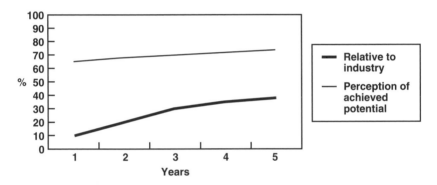

Figure 3.2 Information competency – most firms

warehouse/data mart/data mining activities lull the firm into a false sense of customer competency and progress.

This complacency perpetuates the various 'information kingdoms' within a firm from evolving the degree of information shares. In other words, they do not see the personal benefit to sharing information with their corporate brethren because they do not perceive the added value in doing so. Not only do they not see the added value, they generally perceive it as a potential loss in relative power or a potential threat of being outperformed by the recipient organization. This added to general complacency with the current ability to apply information.

This legacy's persistence also exists because firms attack the problem as an information problem, not as an 'ability to use information' problem. If firms are to regain their intimacy with their customers

and operations, which existed in bygone eras, they must address
their information holistically.

Information and Decision Making – the Art and Science

In pursuit of the understanding of customer information and its
value, it is necessary to understand the role of information in the
context of decision-making.

In early times when the complexity of the business environment was
less, the mechanics of business decisions were quite simple. The
majority of the information resided in the heads of the decision-
makers and those good decisions could be rendered consistently in
the context of mass markets.

As complexity evolved and decision-makers were confounded with
making decisions for business initiatives which demanded more atomic
decisions, they reacted by aggregating the responses, making broader
decisions rather than more decisions. This dynamic masked the impact
of the response because their competitors were reacting in a simpler
fashion. As a result, there were little competitive repercussions.

Another way of viewing this reaction was that the decision-makers
were reacting to increased uncertainty not by increasing the detailed
focus on facts but by aggregating both the growing number of perti-
nent facts and the level of accepted uncertainty.

This is a very human reaction to growing complexity. Physiologically
and psychologically humans have evolved to increasingly grouped
together or 'aggregated' stimuli (facts and uncertainty) in an effort to
effect good decisions in complex environments.

This natural reaction occurs in business too and with relatively little
negative consequence. Now firms are at the market transition phase
where new business imperatives are demanding that 'stimuli' from
customers not be aggregated further. Handling aggregated stimuli
from customers in large corporate environments has grown far
beyond the intellectual capacities of humans. The evolving technologies are starting to provide the capabilities to take on this
tremendous task yet are still in their infancy.

These promising technologies (information machines) can begin the journey toward making good decisions more consistently. The major inhibition is that most humans have a predisposition toward making decisions which rely on information resident in their heads.

One UK banking executive explains his predicament in the change process.

> '. . . People won't say, "My good business decision came from a computer, rather I made a good decision because I'm a smart business person".'

This natural phenomenon also has an influence on a person's perception of actually how a person applied facts to a decision and the relative amount of uncertainty in the same decision.

Humans naturally gravitate toward what is known in a decision rather than focusing on the uncertain aspects of a decision. Thus, their perception of the relative amount of information used to make decisions about their business is distorted by their preoccupation with what they knew about a particular business situation, not what they did not know. When the focus on the 'knowns' (not the 'unknowns') dominates their thinking, it is difficult to make good decisions consistently.

Collected versus Applied

Another critical aspect in understanding the legacy of mass-market customer information is the amount of information which is actually taken in by the firm and how much of that information is applied to actually making decisions.

A typical firm receives a voluminous amount of information. Information is received in all forms and in all manners. The complication is that most information is available to the wrong people, in the wrong form, in the wrong place, and at the wrong time.

Information is generally received by the firm through employees and various types of machines. That information is consequently recorded in human memory, on paper, and in various computers. The ability to access and analyze that information is generally poor because of a host of issues, e.g. political, technological, timing, value perception, and reward structure. At the most points of decision-making, the total sum of information, which was historically collected, and the amount actually applied in decisions, is less than 2%.

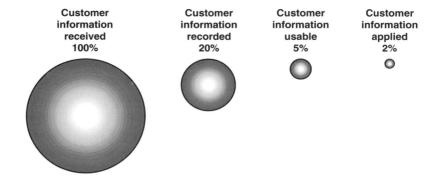

Customer information received 100%   Customer information recorded 20%   Customer information usable 5%   Customer information applied 2%

Figure 3.3   Collected vs. applied customer information

Anatomy of a Customer Decision

Decisions are made up of two primary components: facts and uncertainty. As firms move into atomic information environments, the number of addressable facts increases as well as the amount of addressable uncertainty. Although the increased number of facts is the most apparent change in the decision environment, it is the increase in uncertainty which requires the most attention.

Facts are real. Uncertainty is real. The complication is that uncertainty is often ignored because it is the most difficult component of decision-making. The question then becomes: how does a firm handle uncertainty? To really focus a firm's efforts, the firm must first determine the value of resolving uncertainty, and in particular, which aspects of uncertainty are most worth resolving.

First, it is essential that uncertainty be understood to simply mean the absence of facts in a decision. The amount of uncertainty in almost any decision is inherently far greater than the factual component of a decision. Couple this reality with a decision-maker's predisposition to avoid focusing on uncertainty, and the result is a dysfunctional approach to decision-making. As the decision-maker continues in this manner, the perception develops that the factual component is the predominant part of the decision, not the uncertainty. This is naturally comforting yet inaccurate.

The amount of relative fact and uncertainty addressed in business environments has evolved over the decades in direct proportion to the evolution of complexity in business, creating an environment that demands high aptitude with atomic-level facts, as well as aptitude for a tremendously higher level of uncertainty.

If a firm stopped to objectively model all of the known facts and uncertainty affecting future customer behavior, the analysis would overwhelm most firms.

Customer Knowns vs. Unknowns

When firms stop and divide a decision into percentages of customer knowns and unknowns, they quickly agree that the percentage of unknowns in a typical decision eclipses the percentage of knowns; knowns being facts, unknowns being uncertainties.

Not only do the unknowns eclipse the knowns but only a fraction of the knowns are used in the decision process.

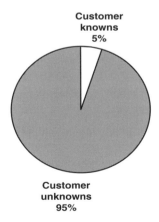

Figure 3.4   Real world business decisions

In addition to the sheer volume of absolute unknowns are the infinite number of relationships between the unknowns and their correlation to predicting future behavior. For example, if a firm targets a certain type of current customer in a direct mail campaign, the list of knowns is quite small relative to all of the information on potential predictors or influences.

The more advanced firms can only claim the following 'knowns' after much work:

+ total customer expenditure/profit;
+ products/services purchased currently;
+ marketing defined customer segment;
+ demographics;
+ likelihood of purchase or response or cross sell;
+ likelihood of defection;
+ previous contact or response.

These knowns and unknowns vary by industry.

Financial Services Industry

Table 3.1 is a chart of the basic (descriptive) knowns for the consumer financial services industry. Although this list is simple, many banks do not apply this very basic information effectively because much of it is aggregated as well as being difficult to access in a timely fashion. But keep in mind, averaged information yields average decisions.

The weakness of the bank's information picture becomes more apparent when all of the information inhibitors are taken into account.

+ Information is aggregated and summarized.
+ Information is not shared between organizations.
+ Much of the information is discarded.

Table 3.1   Understanding customers – banking

Category	Current Customer		Non-Customer	
	Knowns	Unknowns	Knowns	Unknowns
	Customer's name	?		
	Where the customer lives	?		
	Interactions with customer	?		
	Where interactions took place	?		
	Purchased product or service	?		

When banks target non-customers, the unknowns are exponential and thus the proliferation of 'junk mail' is fueled.

The discussion thus far has excluded the implications of sharing customers in the eyes of the shareholders, i.e. information that measures customer profitability. This aspect of information continues to be relatively primitive for most banks.

Telecommunications Industry

The list for the telecommunications industry centers around the details of a call and the details recorded at the switching mechanism, which routes the calls. The list of all potential knowns and unknowns that affect decisions is overwhelming.

Telecommunications firms have similar inhibitors to banks.

✦ Information is aggregated and summarized.
✦ Information is not shared between organizations.
✦ Much of the information is discarded.

Table 3.2   Understanding customers – telecommunications

Category		Current Customer		Non-Customer	
	Knowns	Unknowns	Knowns	Unknowns
	Customer's name	?		
	Where the customer lives	?		
	Interactions with customer	?		
	Where interactions took place	?		
	Purchased product or service	?		
Call	The phone call itself	?		
	Phone number called	?		
	Phone number called from	?		
	Call duration	?		
	Time of day	?		
Switch	The phone call itself (thrown away)	?		
	Intra-later (thrown away)	?		
Billing	Payment history	?		

Retail Industry

The basic list of knowns has actually decreased over the last hundred years in the retail industry as the corner store environment evolved into large multinational organizations with highly diverse customer bases, markets, and resulting logistical complexities. Through this evolution of complexity, retailers were forced to simplify the information they used to drive sales and run operational processes. In terms of decision-making, as the number of variables increased in their business, the ability of the retailer to effectively manage these variables decreased and thus forced them to reduce the number of variables (not truly reducing the uncertainty surrounding the decisions). The approach retailers used to decrease the number of variables was that of summarization and averaging. From a competitive perspective, summarizing and averaging was a non-issue for a long time. If all retailers were forced to summarize seemingly unimportant 'details', the competitive implications would be relatively minor. In addition, previous technologies (mainframes) were unable to process and therefore allow the retailer to utilize this high level of detail. *As information transformation presented itself in the marketplace, the retailers were given the opportunity to get back to the kind of intimate knowledge of customers and operations that was so much a part of retailing in the earlier days.* During the trials of implementation, retailers found their current culture unable to embrace this new culture of information. Thus began the retailers' cultural journey back to their roots.

Today, the list for basic (descriptive) knowns of retailers are distinctively different from both the financial services and telecommunications industry in that there is a conspicuous absence of customer identity. This lack of customer identity is evolving with the advent of retail club areas as well as retailers beginning to use the information revealed when certain payment methods are employed.

Table 3.3 Understanding customers – retail

Category	Knowns	Unknowns	Knowns	Unknowns
Sales	Product	?		
	Store	?		
	Day	?		
	Sales type	?		
	Units	?		
	Revenue	?		
	Cost	?		
	Basket header	?		
	Payment type (check, credit card)	?		
	Total amount	?		
	Shopping basket detail	?		
	Product	?		
	Cash register	?		
	Affinity between products purchased	?		

The link of identity coupled with the affinity relation between products purchased is still a major unknown for most retailers.

The retailer has more transaction-oriented information challenges (e.g. point of sale, inventory). This necessitates predicting behavior of faceless customers with the following complexities:

+ shopping habits;
+ traffic patterns;
+ queues;
+ displays;
+ promotional effectiveness;
+ demographic data;
+ security needs;
+ shrinkage control (shoplifting).

Thus far, the discussion has been confined to descriptive knowns and unknowns. The information picture becomes far more complex with the subject of analytic and predictive knowns and unknowns.

When considering all of the information which could possibly have a bearing on customer behavior and the resulting profitability to shareholders, the list becomes seemingly endless.

Here are only a few:

+ relationships with competitors;
+ relative customer satisfaction with competitors;
+ relative customer satisfaction with non-financial transactions;
+ solicitations from competitors;
+ future life events – births, deaths, marriages, home purchase;
+ timing of other purchase events in the same industry;
+ spending activity in other industries for related products and services;
+ spending activity in other industries for unrelated products and services;
+ travel and recreation events;

- ✦ activities in other industries which are precursors to behavior in retail;
- ✦ personality/moods/weather;
- ✦ physical appearance;
- ✦ personal moral principles.

In order for a business to truly understand the linkage of product and customer, a business should be correlating all these unknowns to each other and other critical issues of price sensitivity, profitability, and the host of risks to the business.

Prioritizing the Value of Knowns and Unknowns

To add further challenge, a firm must decide which knowns and unknowns have the highest rate of return. To do this, there must be a rigorous prioritization of the value-generating potential of all the facts and uncertainties. For most firms, this process is informal and largely arbitrary.

For the firm to really focus their efforts, they must first determine the value of resolving uncertainty, and in particular, which areas of uncertainty are most worth resolving. For example, is it most worthwhile to determine how well the firm satisfied the customer's needs or their competitor's precise customer satisfaction abilities?

Beyond these unknowns is the basic problem of availability of information in a timely fashion. If the information is unavailable to a decision-maker or is available but is not timely, it is still classified as an unknown in a business context. In many cases, much of the information which is currently considered as unavailable is available today; but to the wrong people, in the wrong form, in the wrong place, and at the wrong time.

The Staff Customer Clairvoyant

Firms have been out of touch with the details of their customers for so long that the concept of having customer information similar to that of the sole proprietor one hundred years ago is unfathomable.

To provide a touchstone for the environment which existed one hundred years ago, the concept of the clairvoyant is a helpful metaphor in leading people to think more clearly about just how little they know and the value of increasing the 'knowns' in their business environment. It also sometimes easier to define perfection and then work backwards to the firm's information reality. This concept offers a framework to enable people to think about perfect business knowledge. It gives people the antithesis of their current information position – perfect information. Perfect information about current customers, about potential customers, about their distribution channels, about competitors, about risk, about profitability, and so on.

As part of this thinking exercise, there are several questions that are helpful in bringing the value of customer information to the forefront.

+ What salary would you be willing to pay this clairvoyant to acquire perfect information about customers, competitors' customers, profitability . . .?
+ What level of customer satisfaction could be generated by the clairvoyant?
+ How long would your firm survive if you were competing against a firm with a clairvoyant on staff?
+ How well could its marketing group target your most profitable customers?
+ How well could your firm manage the risks of product availability or logistics?
+ How well could you measure business performance with a clairvoyant?
+ What is the value of having perfect knowledge of customer, product, and distribution channel profitability?
+ How precise could you be at plundering, embracing, cultivating, repelling, and adopting customers, protecting your own, removing the worst, and developing the rest?

Most companies would agree they would have little chance of surviving against such a competitor. As the trade press suggests, many companies are attempting to aggressively develop aspects of these clairvoyant abilities. Armed with the results, they have continued to undertake additional information initiatives, driving them further and faster in the information race.

The Staff Customer Wizard

Next to perfect knowledge is perfect control – the realm of the customer wizard. The wizard is a person with complete control. Suppose this control spans customers, competition, and operations. How much would you pay a wizard to work on your staff? Unlike the clairvoyant who knows exactly what a customer wants or what your competitor's next direct marketing campaign will be, the wizard can make your competitor's store, branch, or switching network disappear or make all of your competitor's customers mysteriously migrate to your firm. What is the value of this complete control?

The relationship between the clairvoyant and wizard concepts and information is this: more useful detail can start the visionaries down the path of clairvoyance (insight) and wizardry (control). If your previous business decisions contained 5% facts, and 95% uncertainty, information mastery could potentially move you to 10% facts, and 90% uncertainty. As you get more proficient with the details, the next step may be 15% facts, and 85% uncertainty. As you continue applying detail, decreasing uncertainty usually increases your level of control – that is, your wizardry. Better information about your business gives you more control over your business and your competitors'.

The Chain Reaction of Intimacy

As firms attempt to break the legacy of mass markets and venture into the world of intimacy, they find a multiplying effect on decisions. In other words, as firms attempt to treat customers as individuals, they are forced into making more decisions.

A world with an increasingly granular decision matrix requires an increasing number of strategies. One leading UK bank executive commented on his firm's cascading challenge:

'In diminishing market segment sizes, the number of segments are skyrocketing, so the dilemma is what and how many strategies do you execute in a massive amount of segments.'

The amount of facts and uncertainty has not risen in such an environment. The corporation has decided to acknowledge their existence. The decision-making process used for aggregated information is inappropriate for the complexities of atomic information. Atomic information also necessitates a more rigorous decision-making process.

4

Litmus Test for Customer Information Mastery

MOST FIRMS UNDERESTIMATE THE TASK OF CREATING CUS-
tomer information competency in their firm and as a result
perceive the amount and area of their investments to be effective and
prudent. This is typically not the case.

To test a firm's customer information competency, every aspect of a
firm's information environment that affects informational effectiveness and efficiency should be taken into account. This includes most
major functional areas, e.g. direct marketing, customer service,
sales.

Effectiveness and Efficiency

Customer information efficiency suggests the exploitation of an improved level of information application in a functional business area
with less time and effort – for instance, subdividing a market by fifty
segments rather than fifteen segments and accomplishing it in half
the time and with half the resources.

The progression of customer information efficiency suggests an increased thrift and quickness with which this new level of information
is employed. An information master could accomplish the same
information-related tasks with five employees in two days compared
to a non-master using fifteen employees for two weeks.

Both effectiveness and efficiency need to be championed by the
entire firm's information community, cognitively as well as emo-
tionally. Both must be present to create this desired environment.

Customer information competency can be divided into three distinct categories: mass market, transitional, and information mastery.

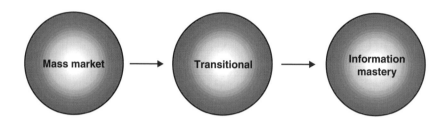

Figure 4.1   Three categories of customer information competency

The first category, mass-market customer information competency, is essentially a firm devoting a majority of its resources to processing transactional oriented information. This task is viewed as an obligatory encumbrance to finish transactional tasks within the firm, e.g. sending out bills, invoices, customer notices.

The second category, transitional customer information competency, is still similar in many respects to the mass-market category, yet this firm has had pockets of success in increasing the level of information sophistication.

The third category, the customer information master, or an 'information-based competitor', is a firm that has devoted a majority of its resources to creating value equally for customers and shareholders. In this category, the firm is capable of creating value for both itself and its customers in an equally beneficial manner. The firm believes that information is truly its most valuable asset and its only sustainable, distinct operational competency.

Most firms are still in the mass-market category. Few firms can claim that information is truly strategically used within their organization.

The chapter will provide firms with a litmus test as to what areas drive information competency, as well as a basic checklist to determine their relative information competency within those areas.

Information competency is defined as the systemic ability to apply any level of information down to the lowest common denominator effectively and efficiently in any situation in servicing customers and shareholders simultaneously.

The totality of information competency is underestimated and under-invested in most firms today. There are seven areas, which will be the framework of the litmus test. They are:

+ people skills;
+ processes;
+ organization structure;
+ culture;
+ leadership;
+ information;
+ technology;

The litmus test contains a series of questions, which offer a checklist approach for any supporting information competency initiative. The litmus test is based on a scale of one to seven, to establish the degree of complement.

People skills

Initiative team's full-time members: Rate 1–7
Mathematician/statistician with excellent industry knowledge
Creative, bright, young, unencumbered thinker
Top business operations person with information and technology
    aptitudes
Top technology person with information and business aptitudes
Internal marketing and public relations person
Executive sponsor with an information vision, political clout, money,
    and tenacity

Processes

There are effective and efficient processes to: Rate 1–7
Share information between business units
Share information between business alliance partners
Apply information at any level of detail
Create, analyze, iterate information centrally
Utilize the lowest level of informational detail
Accurately measure the true condition of the business
Iterate information from customer responses
Retain the majority of learning when consultants are engaged

Organization structure

Our business units/organizations Rate 1–7

Are explicitly rewarded for sharing information between business units upon request

Are explicitly rewarded for proactively sharing information between business units

Are explicitly rewarded for initiating information innovations between business units

Are explicitly rewarded for contributing to the central information of the firm

Do not have stratified layers of information

Integrate very effectively across business and technology groups

Ensure their information is in a form which is very usable by other organizations in the firm

Are structured for optimum information proficiency

Culture

Information Belief System – I believe Rate 1–7

My ability to use information is my most important skill

I will be explicitly rewarded as I improve my information skills

I am explicitly rewarded for applying information in innovative ways

I can access and apply any appropriate information required to service customers

I can access and apply any appropriate information required to service shareholders

Positions centered around information are good for my long-term career

Our firm's heightened focus on information is long term

Our executives encourage some degree of failure in our information initiative

Our executives understand the strategic implications of our firm's information ability

Our firm is fanatical about applying information to service customers and shareholders

Corporate bravery wins explicit rewards

It is seen as OK to 'play a little' with information and its applications

Leadership

Our firm's leadership: Rate 1–7

Has one powerful person who drives our information vision and strategy

Has a sound visionary strategy for applying information

Will be subordinated or be replaced if they block rapid information progress

Are all pushing for world-class information proficiency

Has an accurate understanding of our true information ability

Our information visionary is a:
Leader
Consummate salesperson
Ultimate marketeer
Closet techie
Baggage handler (gets involved at any level)
Circus ringleader
Status quo conspirator
Practicing magician
Accomplished schemer

Information

Rate 1–7

We have ten years of historical information on which to effectively
model
Our information is available at the lowest common denominator
We have one single informal view of the customer, and their
associated profitability
We have one informational financial reality
Most of the firm's information focus is on value creation rather than
administration and control
We can effectively model across economic cycles
Our information allows us to surgically poach, protect, develop, and
remove customers
We have very clean information/data

Technology

Rate 1–7

We have retired all legacy systems which inhibit our information
abilities
We have a central information machine with one version of the truth
Our resources are balanced between decision support and
transactional technologies
Our business cases for technology investments are based on long-term
proficiencies
We have the expertise to implement hybrid transactional and decision
support systems

Corporate culture manifests itself in a firm's approach to information competency.

Customer Information Culture and ROI

These cultural categories have been proven to generate different
degrees of return on investment (ROI) from information competency investments.

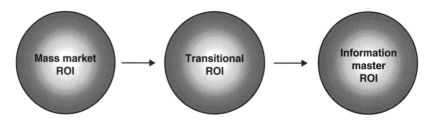

Figure 4.2   ROI from three categories of customer information culture

The first category is defined as a 'mass-market information culture'. This type of culture has the same information fundamentals that businesses have had for the last 20–30 years. Surprisingly, most firms fit into this category. The detailed attributes are described in previous chapters. This type of information culture typically broke even on its information investments.

The second category is termed the 'transitional information culture', firms transforming tactical aspects of their information proficiencies with little systemic transformation. The ROI for this group was typically break-even to ten to fifty times.

The third category is termed an information master or 'information-based competitor culture'. This type of culture is best described as fanatical about information's role in the operations and strategy of their business. The ROI for this group was fifty plus for information investment.

Occasionally, mass-market and transitional firms transcended their ROI categories. This was more a reflection of how primitive their starting point was relative to a small improvement in the spectrum of information ability.

It is also important to recognize that the litmus test for success when measured by conventional return on investment can be misleading. In many cases, the metrics which are not readily measured can have the most impact on customers and shareholders.

If the single test for success in the pursuit of information competency is conventional financial metrics, most firms have succeeded. If a broader and more strategic test is taken in terms of a firm's ability to operate the business at fundamentally a higher level, the majority of firms have failed.

Below is a description of typical admissions from these respective cultures.

Mass-Market Customer Information Cultures

✦ We're not really sure what to do with our customer information.

✦ Customer information is truly not mission critical.

✦ Most of our executives don't understand the value of customer information.

✦ Our business units process customer information efficiently, without being effective (e.g. accounts payable).

✦ When customer information is unavailable, very few people care – business as usual.

Transitional Customer Information Cultures

✦ We're running several customer information-oriented applications but having trouble getting more people to use it.

✦ Some use these customer information applications for some decision-making, but its scope is still fairly narrow.

✦ We have most of the customer information processing power we need.

✦ When customer information is unavailable, one or two groups are upset.

✦ Customer information is not yet mission critical.

✦ Many of our executives really are not sure of the value of the customer information.

✦ We have made some changes on how we use customer information.

Customer Information Mastery Cultures

✦ Corporate culture says if our people do not aggressively apply customer information, they are making bad decisions.

✦ Corporate culture says if users are not using customer information today, they won't be here tomorrow.

✦ Our whole organization believes that we cannot transform fast enough.

✦   We are driving culture with customer information, and the benefits of customer information are driving us.

✦   All of our executives understand the tactical and strategic value of customer information.

✦   We're continually pushing new innovations with customer information.

✦   Our customer information is mission critical today – we can not run our business without it.

It is interesting to note that the information-based competitor firms, although less than a handful in the world, became faster and more committed to their information transformation efforts: speed begets speed.

These fast-moving firms are those who have fostered a culture of learning among employees and executives and have achieved a new awareness of information. These firms have created an environment of information fanaticism. Fanaticism can not be legislated, but created by painstakingly linking the business and personal benefits of applying information in daily work.

It is interesting to note that the bottom third of the firms believed that they were much closer to achieving the high information competency exhibited by the top third of the firms. The reason for this misperception may be that a true understanding of the sophisticated use of information comes only after the firm has actually achieved greater levels of information sophistication. Those firms in the bottom third seemed less aware of their true lack of information sophistication, relative to the information leaders, because they had no method of assessing their situation.

Functional Areas

Beyond the areas of people, process, organization, culture, leadership, information, and technology, traditional functions within a firm each have their own performance metrics for information competency.

Here are some ideas for a general sales and marketing information effectiveness audit:

Customer information effectiveness audit (general)

1 Does your sales and marketing information provide enough detail to direct your marketing group toward the subtle needs and wants of a chosen market?

2 Does your sales and marketing information allow your firm to identify and consequently address the number of micro segments within your market?

3 Does your sales and marketing information allow your firm to effectively analyze a whole marketing system view (suppliers, distribution channels, buying influences, competitors, customers, environment) to plan marketing programs?

4 Does your sales and marketing information allow your company to tightly integrate and coordinate information across major marketing functions?

5 Does your sales and marketing information allow your company to feed meaningful information back to research, manufacturing, purchasing, distribution, and finance?

6 Does your sales and marketing information allow your company to facilitate the new-product development process?

7 Does your sales and marketing information offer accurate feedback of detailed revenue potential and profitability for different segments, customers, territories, products, distribution channels, and order sizes?

8 Does your sales and marketing information provide detailed cost-effectiveness information for sales and marketing expenditures?

9 Does your sales and marketing information allow your company to react effectively to on-the-spot marketing developments?

Here are some ideas for sales and marketing audit directed at a specific industry, like telecommunications:

1 Which customers provide your lowest/highest margins?

2 What is the network option that best suits a particular customer?

3 What are reliable compensation plans based on any combination of customer ABR (average billed revenue)?

4 What impact will competitors' pricing have on your revenue and margins?

5 Which customers are most likely to go to your competition?

6 How is the competition doing in each of your market segments?

7 What impact will new products/services have on revenue and margins?

8 What product and services packages can be built and how will they impact revenue?

10 What sales channel would be most effective for a new product?

11 What is the most effective distribution channel?

12 Which central office features produce the highest/lowest revenue and margins?

5

Historical Approaches for Customer Information Initiatives

INVESTMENTS IN CUSTOMER INFORMATION COMPETENCY HAVE generally been made in technology-oriented areas with some ancillary investment in information itself without investing in systemic abilities of a firm to apply the customer information.

The investment relative to the actual challenges is as follows:

Area	Investment
People	2%
Processes	2%
Organization	2%
Culture	1%
Leadership	1%
Information	10%
Technology	82%
	100%

Investment Myopia

The myopic view of the transformation at hand led to shortsighted investments and insufficient funding. As a result, the project teams found themselves having to go back for funding during the project because they had underestimated the use or scale of the undertaking.

In reality, the project business case procedure is a double-edged sword. If the information visionaries present a project plan that is too extensive, the project may not be sponsored. If the visionaries put forward too small a bid for a project, the project will not receive sufficient financial support to be victorious.

For many visionaries, these types of customer information initiatives had few similar forerunners. As a result, the visionaries had a tricky period approximating appropriate expenditures. One firm's information visionary comments:

> *'We should have put together a complete investment strategy for the total adventure.'*

The visionary continued to say that in this precise situation, articulation of the long-term expenditure is an outstanding instrument for controlling expectations. He commented that without this arrangement:

> *'It is difficult to cope with skyrocketing expectations.'*

This myopia has been consistent throughout the advent of the information machines (technology used primarily for information) in the mid-80s. This capable technology came forward with the ability of processing immense volumes of information, which greatly surpassed the processing capacity of most firms' mainframes. This new technology utilized massive parallel processing to power data warehouses and data marts, and enabled activities such as data mining. This provided firms with the ability to process the enormous quantities of information that were required to execute a customer-focused business model. A number of forward-looking corporations invested in these new 'information machines' while they were still thought of as a corporate and technological gamble relative to the dependable, transaction-based mainframes.

One major incentive for the firms' investment in these information machines was the recognition that their mainframe technology was not intended to handle the enormous detail required to create customer intimacy similar to the quaint corner grocer. As a result, the most vital decisions relating to customers, operations, and financial position were being made in an information void, i.e. there were a great deal of unknowns.

Criteria to Invest

Many corporations based their investments on hurdle rates and business case break-even schedules. Hurdle rates varied from 12% to 21% and break-even periods ranged between six months to five years. These statistics mirror the conventional returns for both technology and non-technology projects. Initial investments for the technology and growth activities span between $1 million and $50 million.

Payback from Customer Information Competency

Many initial sponsors in customer information mastery found payback much higher compared to other technological projects. These early sponsors found great market advantages, thus driving further investment. Many of the early investors make back their investments between six months to two years. The majority of payback time periods were one to four years. The philosophy of the firms on the road to mastery was not the break-even period but the systemic transformation of their firm's information prowess. The near masters reached paybacks of ten to sixty times their original investment.

The surprising comparison was the ROIs from traditional infrastructure, e.g. building, equipment, to this type of investment. The returns from information mastery eclipsed the returns of the traditional investments.

A significant portion of the payback emanated from the firm's new-found ability to respond to variation in the marketplace and react accordingly.

Motivations to Invest

Motivations to invest in information transformation vary from primal competitive fears to a strategic drive to compete at an entirely new level. The motivation varied based on the relative competitive timing of the investment.

Early on, investors acknowledged that competitive lead was their main ambition. They saw customer information mastery as a means to gain market share and operational efficiency. Investors who jumped in later on did so largely out of market trepidation.

Market Advantage vs. Market Requirement

Market advantages were referred to as the basic motive for early investors. These corporations believed that they could benefit in terms of customer share and logistical competence. The firms that invested later on did so out of apprehension of being out maneuvered by firms with greater information capabilities. One large US retail executive states that:

> '*We kept reading about our competitors doing similar things, so we jumped in because of our competitor anxiety.*'

This firm could only look on as their competitors took their best customers because they didn't have the information to stop them.

This figure illustrates the progression of a firm's thinking relative to how they perceived their need for information mastery relative to a 'must have' and a 'nice to have' competitive competency.

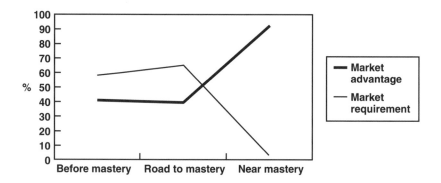

Figure 5.1　Market advantage vs. market requirement

Revenue Creation vs. Cost Avoidance

Most corporations were driven by the opportunity to significantly increase new revenue in a shrinking marketplace. As they continued on their road to mastery, the opportunities to become very sophistic-ated with their distribution channels made them aware that oper-ational efficiencies could be very significant given a more sophisticated information approach.

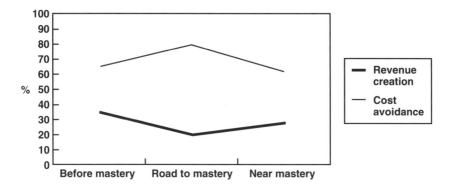

Figure 5.2   Revenue creation vs. cost avoidance

Identifying the best customers to acquire was the significant part of how firms applied their new levels of information competencies. The wisdom gained from the scrutiny of profitability factors then drove marketing strategy. Nearly 22% of a firm's customers represented high revenue creation potential, while 78% of the customers repres-ented moderate revenue opportunities.

Immediate Impact vs. Long-Term Focus

Most firms realized that their information investments in mastery were for the long haul. There seems to be a temptation for the firms to shift their focus toward the short term after they had a taste of short-term profits. This shift was risky because real systemic pro-gress was put in jeopardy.

In reality, quick project wins are necessary for a project's continued existence, although a balance with the long-term objectives must be maintained to achieve the big gains promised by systemic change.

Business Case for Customer Information Mastery

The business case for the road to mastery is the foundation upon which a corporation perceives the project's future value. In addition, the ambiguity associated with new systemic information investments is inherently difficult to quantify and readily articulate in a traditional business case. This is especially true when competing against traditional 'tried and true' technology investments. The heritage of badly implemented business case methods has made the process dubious at best. Portraying the business case as a realistic forecast of forthcoming payback for the purpose of securing backing from the corporate patrons proved to be more difficult than anticipated.

The information visionaries in the firm were at the center of the business case process. These visionaries had the drive and vision to understand the potential benefits and hence the elements of the business case which would be most compelling. In order to execute this vision, they had to secure the funds, which meant convincing the corporate sponsors that the benefits outweighed the costs.

The Business Case Game

Acquiring finances for the road to information mastery had the same processes for other initiatives, which contained overstated benefits. This overstatement cast a shadow on the benefits forecast for this critical project. As such, the holders of corporate funding collectively would raise their payback goals to compensate for overplayed benefits. This results in a distorted view of benefits and actual payback. If the information initiative seems to be debatable or unappealing, the business case team is told to adjust numbers and expenses downward. This causes suspicion and mistrust from all levels of management.

Unfortunately, many firms didn't realize that the investment in information mastery reliably developed strong payback, typically outshining most other investments. This chaos instigates insufficient project funding, deferment, or the decision to invest in predictable technologies. The source of the overstatement comes from the deficiency in precise business-case processes. Without these processes, a genuine payback is not viable and the actual worth is masked.

Firms have advanced business cases traditionally to rationalize a prior conclusion, rather than meticulously contrast viable options represented at median values. They also have neglected to overtly depict the downside risk of the project as well. One UK banking executive commented:

> '. . . Our joke is that if a project is strategic, it has a lot of zeros after it.'

It is difficult to estimate potential payback of future business opportunities created by information mastery. As one high street UK banking executive states:

> 'We began with a preconceived notion of the benefits array and ended up with benefits coming from completely different areas . . . areas we never would have planned on.'

The firm could not have predicted the new prospects as they weren't thinking enough about them, nor did they even know of their existence.

Another area which is not easy to predict is the future value of learning. As another UK banking executive stated:

> 'Better information gives better learning.'

Learning is one of the major values of information competency, yet does not end up as a quantified piece of the business case very often.

The studies showed that the short-term payback of information mastery was insignificant compared to the total impact of increasing a firm's systemic ability to apply information across its business. The strategic impact of information mastery is difficult to measure and many times overlooked as the major aspect of customer information competency. Therefore, if information mastery is viewed as short-term, the overall impact is likely to be less.

Initiatives in customer information mastery, by their temperament, are uncharacteristic of many initiatives. Traditional employees are on edge when viewing a project that they may have to justify over financial reporting cycles of a firm. Many projects were masquer-aded as more conventional undertakings to solve more easily under-stood challenges within a firm. Many information mastery projects had to be implemented very quietly so as to give them time to prove their value before the factions of traditional thinkers could rally to halt its progress.

Many customer information mastery initiatives had preliminary tests of value as part of proving their value to the firm. The value verified by the test usually was enough to sustain the preliminary investment.

One leading UK bank gave an example of their pilot in six retail locations. At the conclusion of the pilot, the firm was able to deter-mine that marketing response rates in these six stores had doubled during the period. In this particular case, the firm applied detailed customer-behavior/demographic information to model propensity to purchase certain industry products.

A major US bank was able to demonstrate calculable value from small improvements in the elements of information mastery. These components included increases in revenue, employee savings, mail-ing, productivity of operations, and technology savings. Qualitative elements such as customer satisfaction and overall improvement in the firm's ability to be flexible were deemed to have the largest impact yet they were more difficult to quantify. Although the figure below shows qualitative impacts higher than quantitative impacts, the quantitative impacts dwarfed more traditional projects' total impact.

Organizational Involvement

Traditional business functions of marketing, sales, service, and the traditional organizations of technology (IT) were both involved in the information mastery initiatives. Although IT was only 10%

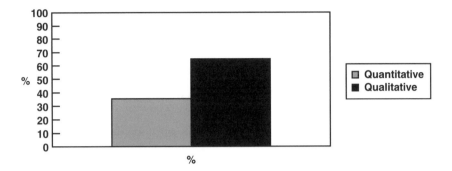

Figure 5.3   Qualitative vs. quantitative benefits

of the determinants of value of a broad customer information competency, they were heavily involved because of the traditional perception that IT competency was synonymous with information competency. As firms continued on the road to mastery, the realization of IT's role became clearer and the role of the business functions increased.

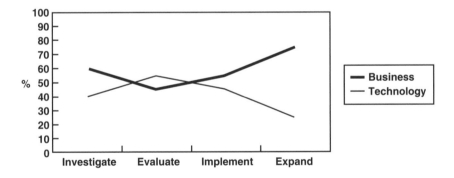

Figure 5.4   Organizational involvement

Investment Criteria

Most firms have certain criteria for investments in traditional projects. Those same criteria were applied to decisions in customer information mastery projects. Payback, internal rate of returns, return on investments, and return on assets were typical. Rates of return varied from 12% to 20% and payback periods extended from six months to three years. Preliminary investments for information initiatives extended from $2 million to $60 million.

Motivations to Invest and Expand

Motivation prompting customer information investments reflects both the internal and external forces driving the firms to take action. The impetus to invest has changed from firms seeking competitive advantage to a competitive necessity in order to maintain market share and profitability in any marketplace.

The first step was to ask firms about their reasons for investing in information transformation, and how those rationales evolved throughout the purchasing and expansion stages.

Competitive Advantage vs. Competitive Necessity

Many of the firms in the research were considered early adopters, and they clearly invested in the technology for the purpose of gaining competitive advantage. Seventy two percent of the motivation to invest was to gain competitive advantage, and when the time came to expand their investment in customer information transformation, 82% of the motivation was to keep the lead and possibly expand that lead.

Figure 5.5   Motivation: initial investment vs. expansion

These firms tended to have one individual or a group of individuals who were visionary about the use of customer information:

> *Those who do not master customer information will be mastered by those who do.*

Sales vs. Operational

Early understanding of customer information's impact on sales was evident by responses. Firms stated that 75% of their motivation to invest was driven by their desire to drive sales through the use of detailed information. Twenty five percent of the motivation was operationally oriented. When firms were asked why they had expanded or why they would expand their systems, they stated that 81% of their motivation was still sales oriented, with 19% being operationally oriented.

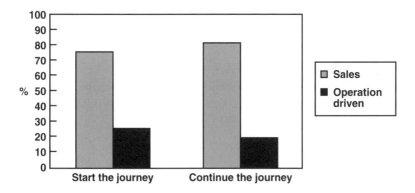

Figure 5.6   Sales driven vs. operations driven

Information vs. Process

The firms' response to a similar motivational question was quite different. When asked if they invested in the customer information technology purely for information or to support processes, the firms stated that 72% of the motivation was informational; only 28% of the motivation was to support processes. When asked about the motivation to expand, the answer changed. The information motivation was now only 55% and 45% to use the information to support processes.

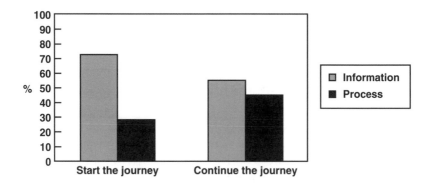

Figure 5.7   Information driven vs. process driven

This shift symbolized the learning that had taken place relative to detailed information's major bottom-line impact on efficiency and effectiveness.

Firms were beginning to learn that they could reduce costs significantly with a detailed understanding of processes. This learning furthered their understanding of the significant implications to core processes, and caused (sometimes forced) them to re-examine and potentially completely eliminate some long-standing operational practices.

Short term vs. Long term

Firms clearly indicated that 60% of the motivation to invest in customer information transformation was long-term focused with 40% being short-term focused.

Many firms accepted customer information as a fundamental, competitive evolution in the retail industry, and felt that they would rather be ahead of the power curve. With this long-term decision in mind, they still expected short-term results with their bottom line.

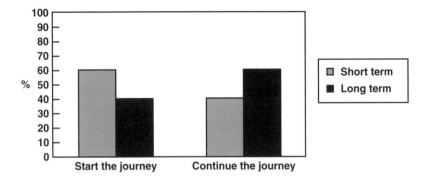

Figure 5.8   Purchase drivers: short term vs. long term

Internal Business Case for Customer Information

For visionaries, the elements of a customer information business case were typically centered on sales and marketing issues. Other areas that were common are as follows:

✦ channel effectiveness;
✦ profitability;
✦ contact management;
✦ attrition;
✦ fee management.

For retailers, the elements of customer information business cases varied by the firm. Some of the elements estimated in the business cases were the following:

✦ increased sales through out-of-stock;
✦ increased profits through better sell-thru;
✦ increased stock turns through identifying slow-moving items;
✦ decreased markdowns;
✦ better negotiations;
✦ better stock allocation and acquisition;

+ increased overall margin;
+ reduction in staff hours per store.

For telecommunications firms, the elements of customer information transformation business cases again focused around sales and marketing. Other elements common were:

+ contact management;
+ network optimization;
+ fraud detection;
+ propensity to buy.

A Question of Business Case Competency

Examining the internal business cases for customer information yielded consistently low business-case competencies for these banks compared to other industries. The lack of specialized skills and processes to do world-class business cases was noticeable in most of the banks. With respect to the value of customer information technology, the investment has proven to be a stellar one for most banks.

If it is any consolation, few people or organizations in any industry studied received high marks in the business-case category. The reasons are simple. Most organizations' business-case approach is doomed from the start.

Organizations typically approach a business case not to create and compare all feasible strategies represented at median values. Nor do they generally have any explicit representation of downside risk. The business case is generally used to justify a decision, made after the fact. This is okay if the firm always makes good decisions. If the initiative is contentious, business case preparers are asked to shift the numbers up or down depending on the desired goals, not the facts of the decision. As a learned response to these practices, senior management has learned to distrust business cases and consequently set unrealistically high criteria in response. In doing so, many truly strategic and critically important investments are bypassed for more tactical and, many times, less impactful investments over the long term.

Clearly, good outcomes are what we like; yet good decisions are the best we can do. And the best way to get good outcomes is to make good decisions.

Therefore, preparing realistic business cases that reflect the uncertainty, upside and downside of each decision strategy is most desirable. Building quality business cases requires decision-makers and staff to work as a team and not as adversaries.

Interestingly enough, the absence of sound business-case approaches in the firms' information transformation process did not keep them from an excellent outcome: high ROI.

Investment Drivers

In terms of investment drivers, more firms were driven by short-term issues to begin their journey. As they began to understand the broad implications of a systemic customer information competency, their focus became longer term.

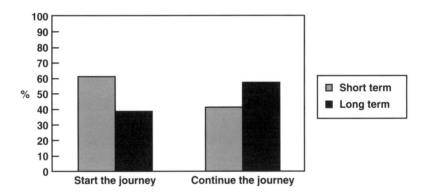

Figure 5.9   Investment drivers

Business Case Process

For those firms who are still struggling with the business case for investing in customer information, their lack of business-case competence could cost them precious time and forestall making a strategic customer information. When asked about their business-case process, the firms stated that 55% of their business-case process was less formal whereas 45% of their business-case process was more formal.

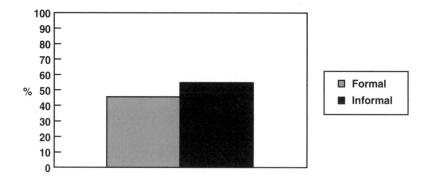

Figure 5.10   Business case process

There are two reasons for this mix. Most organizations did not have the time, experience, and resources available to develop a robust business case. Secondly, the 'gut feel' that this technology would be the basis for competing in the retail industry over the next ten years dominated their thinking.

In terms of quantitative vs. qualitative elements, firms responded that only 35% of the business case was quantitative and 65% of the business case was qualitative.

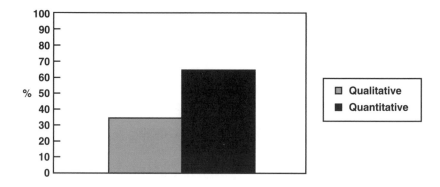

Figure 5.11   Qualitative vs. quantitative

When asked whether the business case was short-term oriented or long-term oriented, firms responded by stating that roughly 40% of the business case was short-term oriented and 60% was long-term oriented.

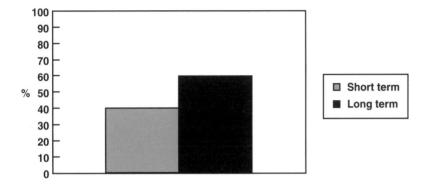

Figure 5.12   Business case timeframe balance

6

Seven Elements of Customer Information Competency

IN THE TUMULTUOUS STRUGGLE TO DRAG THEIR FIRMS FROM the clutches of their mass-market customer information legacy, information visionaries found seven areas which not only represented the primary gauntlets to information transformation but were also the keys to achieving world-class customer information competency. These areas could be categorized as: people, processes, organization, culture, leadership, information, and technology.

In order to make fundamental changes to the way the firm applied information, they would have to address deep-seated customer information legacies. For the most part, firms have failed to make the fundamental changes in the broad and deep competency of applying information because of these legacies.

While most firms acknowledge they have moved further into a true customer-focused business model, they realized they had gradually lost touch with the true value of information. As a result, they no longer had a clear understanding of what it takes to create a robust information environment.

The path to becoming the world's leading information master brought them face-to-face with their most daunting nemesis – themselves. In essence, this discovery process availed a telling and sometimes disturbing corporate X-ray.

The customer information competency iceberg

Many of the insights shared by the visionaries who have been a part of their firm's quest to become the world's most informed competitor were hidden until implementation brought them to the surface.

The challenges that arise when confronting a firm's customer information legacy are analogous to an iceberg. When the object is initially sighted, only 10% of the object is visible. This 10%, which is visible, is generally regarded to be technology and information itself. The unseen 90% is the mass-market legacy of people, processes, organizations, culture, and leadership. The 100% can be divided into seven categories – people, processes, organization, culture, leadership, information, and technology. Using the iceberg analogy, most of the firms invested 90% of their capital and resources in the visible portion of the iceberg. As a result, 90% of the actual challenge went unnoticed. It was only when the firm ventured further into their transformation efforts that the submerged portion of the iceberg made itself known to them.

Although a primary enabler in this race is technology (information machines), the majority of critical elements are non-technological in nature. Central to this transformation is the firm's ability to change the traditional epicenters of power and politics.

In the analogy, the explicit investment represents the visible portion of the iceberg. The challenge represents the submerged portion of the iceberg.

In terms of percentages, the McKean Paradox reveals the historical information investments relative to the information competency determinants in most firms shown in Table 6.1.

It is this weighting that has caught most of the firms off guard in terms of the real challenges they face in transforming themselves. It is important to note that the technological issues are quite daunting in their own right as they represent new competencies for corporate computing. It is the non-technological issues which have kept most of the firms from transforming themselves into the information firm of tomorrow.

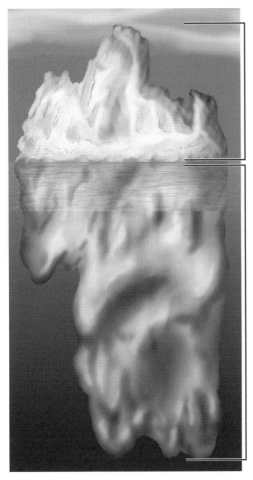

Most firms invest in traditional functions and activities:
- marketing
- sales
- service
- loyalty schemes
- technology

The majority of the challenge lies in areas more difficult to acknowledge, change and secure long-term changes:
- people's advanced information skills
- legacy mass-market processes
- organizational information autonomy
- information culture/belief
- senior executive awareness/engagement
- quality information at the lowest common denominator

Figure 6.1   The customer information competency iceberg

People

One of the most important issues in the implementation of any major information initiative is the people who work in the customer information project. Much of the discussion ultimately revolved around the personnel challenges. The skills, attitudes and paradigms within which each firm operated had a profound impact on all aspects of the information initiative. In most projects, the skills and personnel required were underestimated and consequently under-resourced.

Table 6.1   Historical customer information investments

Area	Historical Customer Information Investments	Customer Information Competency Determinants
People	2%	20%
Process	2%	15%
Organization	2%	10%
Culture	1%	20%
Leadership	1%	10%
Information	10%	15%
Technology	82%	10%
TOTAL	100%	100%

In fact, most of the firms cited personnel challenges as being the single biggest obstacle to success. In most cases, there was no specific plan to address the personnel issue.

The people issue, which made up roughly 20% of the total transformation challenge, virtually went unaddressed.

People skills

Firms quickly found that their people did not have the information skill levels equal to the levels of information capabilities they were planning to provide. The skills that were lacking extended from sophisticated analysis skills to applying information made available to call-center employees. One major US retailer gives his view.

'. . . We build all this information technology capability, and our people either didn't believe it really worked, were scared of it, or didn't have the skills to really apply it.'

Many firms developed the technological piece of their information competency and expected that the people would naturally gravitate to developing the incentives for people to encourage employees to 'want to be part of that information stuff'. This UK banking executive states:

'. . . Our firm always encouraged a particular set of skills that our firm rewarded people for, which had little to do with the information skill sets for the future.'

Many firms lurched forward with information initiatives that their people couldn't fully exploit. For example, if a firm implemented a sophisticated sales information network, but the sales people were afraid to use it because they were insecure about their information technology abilities, the impact of the initiative is limited. In addition, if the sales people's skills afford a basic use of the information sales system and the firm does not cultivate an environment for further skill development, the potential impact is truncated.

One US banking executive commented:

'. . . We need salespeople who can handle the more advanced use of customer information.'

The absence of base-line information proficiency will not only curtail current business functions but also reduce the ability to discover new future opportunities.

The need for mathematics

Mathematics is a functional aspect of information mastery. Math is the key to unlocking the meanings of information. Many firms found that such mathematical and statistical skills were conspicuously absent in their firm.

Firms found that they just could not hire people with good mathematical or statistical skills to create value from their information. The skills of mathematicians and statisticians had to be acclimated to the information environment.

One major US retailing executive made comments such as:

'We should have hired a boat full of statisticians.'

Others commented that:

'Math is the key to understanding information.'

Beyond the new information skills of specialized mathematics, analysis, and modeling, highly advanced relational database skills were required. In most cases, these types of skills were almost non-existent. There was no compelling reason for them to exist in a mass-market environment. Often, there may have been individuals within the organizations who had the appropriate skills, which could be adapted to this new environment, but were reluctant to enter into this relatively unknown information environment, an environment viewed as radical and unproven, with the stigma of being a high-risk career move. Very talented candidates would simply not be interested in venturing into this unknown assignment because it would interfere with their current fast track to the next management assignment.

The need for mathematics in the retail industry offers special challenges to information competency. Firms came to realize that the use of dynamic statistical business models has a strong effect on the payback of the applied information. In hindsight, they learned that without dynamic business models, simply relying on historical forecasting, the only environment they could accurately predict was one that did not require any changes in variables. For example, in a retailer's environment, the following variables would have to remain constant for historical modeling to be effective:

+ demand;
+ price;
+ seasonality;
+ promotion style;
+ competition;
+ weather;
+ no significant random variances in sales.

This is a highly unlikely scenario. As one renegade explained, a statistician who knows statistics is helpful, but when a statistician understands the retail business, the payback can be significant.

Barriers to information skill advancement

Many firms found that their environment for information skill advancement was inhibited by the legacies of how the firm values information and the skills to apply it.

Elasticity, candidness and originality are an essential part of developing the skills for information mastery, yet typically the environment containing these attributes did not exist in many of the firms.

One UK banking executive commented '. . . candidness, collaboration and open-mindedness were not traits our firm encouraged'.

Not only are they not encouraged, but also there is no explicit reward structure to support them.

Reluctant to engage

Many firms found that their employees were hesitant to join the journey toward information mastery because they believed that this type of work would cast them as a certain type of employee with a limited career path.

One major US retailing executive explains:

> *'Our people viewed these information skills as technology specific and they perceived that as not helping them for their marketing or sales career.'*

One visionary characterized many of the employee responses as:

> *'Sorry, I am waiting for my next marketing promotion.'*

Several of the firms learned how to develop a change in attitude to combat this resistance to joining the journey to information mastery. They put in place specific rewards, which were high profile with top executives publicly announcing and supporting their central role.

Another resistant stemmed from the fact that information skills were viewed as something similar to a programming skill, which would be low value and commonplace in the corporate employee pool.

One US telecommunications executive echoed this by stating:

> *'People initially viewed these skills as inherent "techie" which*
> *they had no interest in pursuing.'*

And when an employee is a 'techie', they perceive that they will always be viewed as a 'techie'.

An environment of experimentation

Many firms did not have the environment to experiment with the information – a key part of discovering new opportunities.

Many times the firm would have set up the rich information environment and then placed tight restrictions on its use and accountability.

One major US telecommunications executive comments:

> *'We created this great information environment and then we*
> *put a toll-booth on its usage – what a mistake!'*

Employees from a non-technology era

Employees, who spent much of their career not surrounded by technology, felt very resistant to joining the journey to mastery because of the requirement to use technology in some form or fashion.

Many of the employees still had not come to grips with technology and did not want to deal with the skills necessary to exploit the information. Their inability to use technology is not necessarily age-related. It is more a factor of their attachment to the past. It is this attachment that keeps them clinging to their approaches of yesterday, and holds them forever in the past. In many cases, the most intense training program will not change the culture or thinking of these employees of a legacy approach. It is just a natural evolution of business that will prompt them to move to the sidelines.

Under duress, others had reluctantly used the technology only as required. Some, as a consequence of their background and nature, had immersed themselves in the 'art of the possible' with technology.

Beyond the issue of skill sets is the 'customer information generation' the person has spent most of their working career in. As with most firms, there are different types of people within the organization with differing relative competencies. People who have spent most of their time in the mass-market information generation are tuned to aggregated information usage. In the new information environment, it is helpful to consider people's information generation when assessing the transformation efforts. It appeared that people could be grouped into three basic information generations – Info-phobics, Info-transitionals, and Info-babies.

Figure 6.2   Customer information generations

These generations align with the phases of customer information competency.

Figure 6.3   Phases of customer information competency

Info-phobics

Info-phobics are those who have a fear of using customer information beyond a mass-market approach. They practice avoidance behavior when confronted with the decision to use or not use information in a more sophisticated manner. They typically focus on the risks of using information rather than the innovations and the resulting rewards.

Intertwined with the info-phobia is a fear of technology. Employees that are scared of technology feel that it will either take their job or make them feel silly or not intelligent. This generation is the most challenging because they are grounded in the past yet have the aptitude to accomplish the task at hand.

Info-transitionals

Info-transitionals are those who are on the borderline between the old and new worlds. They typically have the aptitude for the new world but are tied to the old world by tradition and current beliefs. With training and encouragement, they could leave their current customer information legacy with little difficulty.

In this generation, technology is seen as the enemy. In many cases they had the intellectual capability to exploit the technology, but it is their overriding attitude which hampers them.

Info-babies

Info-babies hold the future of customer information in their hands. Doing things differently and doing different things with customer information is playtime to them. Customer information is the new art of their industry. They see the world through the innovations of customer information rather than comparing how things had always been done in the past.

The last group of 'info-babies' regard technology as an extension of themselves. Customer information mastery represented to them the new art of business and the only way to move into the future.

Consultants

An important aspect of achieving customer information mastery is the use of consultants. They can potentially be a great help, yet their value depends on how much learning the firm can do while it is engaging these consultants in their areas of expertise.

In many cases, the consultants end up leaving with most of the knowledge because the firm has not set up an environment to learn from the consultants.

It is critical that a delicate balance is created when engaging consultants. It is important to keep in mind that the objective is to create a long-term competency rather than achieve a tactical end state.

One US retailing executive expresses his misgivings after his firm realizes that the consultants were much smarter, not his firm:

> *'We finished our first implementation and realized we were no more smarter about using our information yet the consultants were . . .'*

The personality factor

It was clear that the type of person that the firm needs to stick with this information initiative must have a great deal of stamina and energy. There was a high degree of project exhaustion from people who were working tremendous hours with insufficient support and resources to accomplish the task. In many cases because these projects were not mainstream and regarded as experimental, the pressures were accentuated. This also affected their ability to recruit top-notch people to the project.

One Australian bank executive explains:

> *'The attrition of people on the project is extremely high because we were forever breaking new ground and fighting the conventional powers in our firm who were dead set against it.'*

This roadblock could have been helped by powerful, overt recognition from the firm's infrastructure. The profiles of personnel and cultural issues may also have revealed unreasonable expectations on the part of the firms. This syndrome is endemic in information technology projects. The volume of work, the time allocated, and the available resources may be unrealistic for firms keen to keep ahead of the competition.

The inherent nature of new information initiatives requires people who are comfortable with a higher degree of risk. These projects are usually outside corporate norms. They tend to tread on the hallowed ground of powerful factions dead set against change. After all,

information is inextricably linked to power. Power has been traditionally derived from information legacies. As a result, many of the
people with the right skill sets do not join the new information
initiatives because of their inherent aversion to risk. In the case of the
visionary, most chose to carry forward the information torch partly
because of their comfort with high-risk career activities.

Aptitude

In many cases, the inherent aptitude of the people using customer
information on a day-to-day basis was compatible with mass-market
information approaches. For example, a person who previously re-
lied on using general information reports to serve customers may not
have the aptitude to use more sophisticated 'what if' tools in the
pursuit of understanding potential customer behavior.

Processes

Most firms found that when they went to a new level of detail and
sophistication with their customer information, the information processes were no longer efficient and in some cases completely invalid.

There were several factors involved in this change:

✦ The source of the customer information changed.

✦ The level of detail available changed the inherent process.

✦ The new customer information changed the strategy, which further changed processes.

✦ Acquiring the right customer information changed its
  application.

✦ The new customer information changed the management process.

✦ The new customer information changed the measurement process.

✦ New customer information applied to customers changed the
  customers' behavior.

✦ New customer information changed the speed of the process.

✦ Availability of customer information changed the organizations
  involved in a given process.

✦ Availability of customer information completely erased a process.

✦ Availability of customer information added a process.

Customer information's operational implications

One of the most underestimated issues of customer information was the lack of consideration of the process by which information is applied by people – its form, its flow, and its evolving iteration with use. As such, the overall understanding of information's effect on a firm's operational effectiveness and efficiency was almost non-existent.

Firms said that 80% of the motivation to invest in information transformation was driven solely by the need for information. Only 20% of the motivation to invest in information transformation was process oriented.

Most firms changed their preconceptions after actually moving into the transformation. For some firms focus shifted dramatically once they experienced the power of a new level of detail and insight. When asked why they would expand their information transformation efforts, they responded that 55% of the motivation to expand their information transformation was driven by need for information and now 45% of the motivation was driven by the application of information to processes.

Why did this focus shift? As firms summarized customer nuances, they also summarized process or operational nuances. The result was the same: dollars were being lost in the operational details.

The firms had found that they could apply detail in two areas:

1 Use of detailed information to *manage* processes or operations, and

2 Use of detailed information to *model* world-class processes.

Managing processes with information

Transforming a firm's mass-market information environment has significant implications for how processes are managed. The research firms found that the less aggregated information approaches (more detailed levels of information) led to an enhanced ability to manage processes. This was due to the fact that managing aggregated information with more aggregated information leads to a tremendous level of uncertainty surrounding operations.

This was particularly true in the retail industry with a great deal of sophistication in the logistics for predictive replenishment. Retailers are known to say:

'Retail is Detail', or 'the dollars are in the detail.'

In order to extract the 'dollars', a true understanding of operations and logistics can only be achieved through atomic levels of information.

One major US retailer in the research found $10 million hidden in the previously summarized information from logistical efficiencies from only one line of merchandise. Using sophisticated information techniques, the merchandisers were able to optimize their warehousing strategy for one line, save bottom-line costs in shipping, and negotiate additional warehousing discounts. This was just one aspect of the logistics of getting this line to the right customers, at the right price, at the right time, and without the assistance of the technology group, as would previously have been the case.

If this level of information were applied to all levels of efficiency in all merchandise within this product line, the payback would be exponential. The retailers found that the bottom-line impact of managing an entire logistical path at this level of 'scientific' detail yields tremendous cost efficiencies.

Only a handful of retailers even entered this world of atomic detail for logistics. These retailers did find staggering payback and say that it is just the beginning. The added managing detail increased efficiency.

The retailers who attempted to apply this new level of detail to process effectiveness and efficiency found old processes inefficient and invalid given the new information environment. For the few retailers who did reach this point of information transformation, there were unanticipated challenges regarding processes, which had been efficient enough under the previous information environment. Three process scenarios seemed to occur.

1 A traditionally efficient process using aggregated information was no longer needed.
2 A traditionally efficient process using aggregated information needed modification to more effectively utilize the detail.
3 An entirely new process was needed.

One retailer recounts the realization that information transformation holds unanticipated process transformations. The major US retailing executive states:

> *'The biggest benefit of the detail was now driving our biggest retailing challenge.'*

Optimizing operations for iterative decision-making

Another important aspect of utilizing the detail in processes is the ability to iteratively make operational decisions. The ability to apply iterative decisions to business is a key aspect of information transformation. In other words, it is important to test business hypotheses prior to full commitment. In a sense, the new information environments should provide a type of option value – giving the firm the option not to fully commit to a major business initiative without iteratively testing a hypothesis – technology's version of puts and calls from the financial markets.

Modeling new and existing processes through information

In the research, it was clear that only a few retailers had reached the point of starting to actually use the detail to model new world-class processes. Most firms realized that the new information environment not only allowed them to do things differently, but also allowed them to do different things. One retailer viewed the information transformation as allowing them to expand their thinking for their value chain. This includes the creation of new processes as well as modifying existing processes with information. The concept of continuous process improvement fits extremely well with information environments, which provides the speed and flexibility to change the ongoing process.

The new information transformation also enables incremental action, and cuts down tremendously on the cycle time for answering smaller and more frequent questions.

Most transforming firms have received high payback from this reduced cycle time in terms of competitive response and adjusting business decisions on the fly. As the iterative decision-making capability has given retailers tremendous sales improvements, this same ability will produce tremendous long-term payback for continuous process improvement programs. This new type of information environment allows TQM (total quality management).

Organizations

The structure of the organization can inhibit a firm's ability to transform its customer information legacy. Most firms came to the realization that the organizational aspects of information held back their efforts to restructure their basic form and function.

Structure

Most of the firms observed that the current organizational structure of their firm was well suited for mass-market approaches to customer information application but not for atomic information applications. Such acknowledgements hold the fundamental changes the firms have to make in order to become viable competitors in the future.

Many firms remarked that their efforts towards customer information mastery heightened their awareness that sales and service must be linked informationally. A US banking executive commented on the necessity to:

'Totally change their marketing structure.'

One major UK banking executive surmised that in order to move towards customer information mastery, their firm had to undertake a:

'Radical destruction of corporate kingdoms which existed for personal gain and echo rather than for the good of the firm.'

Semi-autonomous business units

One of the structural problems experienced was inherent in the composition of the organization. Firms typically were not just one homogenous company but a collage of semi-autonomous units, which acted in response to a gamut of disparate agendas. One leading US banking executive stated:

'Each business unit has their own technology support and that keeps us operating like six competitors.'

In this case, each of their business units has no direct incentive to share customer information between the units. In addition, they don't have the additional resources to share it.

This scenario is very typical of firms trying to master the art of information competency. Their existing information competency is usually segmented by either business unit or functional units. This environment keeps them from gaining synergy from working together in order to achieve a greater power from their information. Unfortunately, the business silos that exist are held together by many years of tradition and power. It is only when devastating business environments cause change or powerful, visionary executives enter the picture that these segmented environments are given an opportunity to change.

This major US retailer commented that:

'After we had managed to implement the beginnings of a strong information competency did we see the impact it had on our segmented approach to business. All of a sudden, it was easy to share information and everyone could see the benefit to do so.'

Organizational evolution of support

Support for information initiatives was not broad or deep enough to accomplish significant transformation for most of the firms. The support of information initiatives was tracked at three different levels within the firms: executives, management and general employees.

The quest for information mastery was supported at varying levels within the corporation. In general, most levels within the corporation became more supportive as they saw the potential impact this type of environment would have on them personally as well as professionally.

Evolution of organizational support by level

This first section shows the results of research of consumer-intensive industries in which the information transformation was plagued by great cultural challenges.

Financial services industry

Senior management support. The highest level within the corporation was probably the most critical in supporting the efforts to create information mastery. It was clear that there was a tremendous stratification of support even at the executive level of most firms. In general, it appeared that there was a small faction of supporters who were more visionary in nature, yet the majority were either neutral or resistant. This makeup of supporters and non-supporters in the ranks of the executives was brought on by the fears of uncertainty as well as the unconventional nature of such initiatives.

The firms reported that a small percentage of senior management put their backing behind the initiative. Most of the senior management adopted a 'wait and see' attitude. This attitude emanated from the perception that failure of this type of initiative would have tremendous political consequences within the firm. Other senior management just didn't understand the broad implications of developing a systemic information competency.

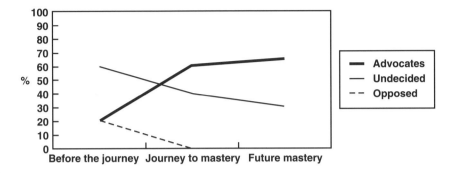

Figure 6.4   Evolution of senior management support in banking

Middle management support. Middle management exhibited similar support patterns for customer information initiatives, as did senior management.

As with executives, the same percentage of middle managers supported the initiative as resisted it. The middle managers started out slow in terms of supporting the initial information initiative. The percentage of middle managers that were undecided remained high until the project was well under way. As with executives, middle managers' support increased radically as the project showed signs of success.

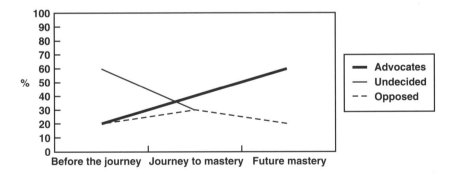

Figure 6.5   Evolution of middle management support in banking

General employee support. General employee support was quite different than that of senior management and middle management. For the most part, they were undecided because they were not actively involved in the project in the early stages. It is ironic that the majority of people who will implement this capability were not involved early on. Most people felt that the support of the general employee would advance as they began to see the impact this capability would have on their work.

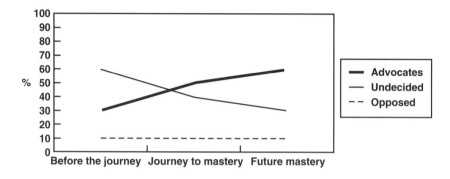

Figure 6.6   General employee support in banking

Retail industry

Senior management support. The level of organizational support in retail differed from the financial services industry in that retailers were generally more respectful of the competitive edge information competency brought them. It was interesting to track the evolution of support of information transformation from the early stages of interest through implementation, and ask the retailers to project that support into the future. During the early stages, these primarily 'earlier adopter' firms have the level of support from senior management within the sphere of involvement shown in Figure 6.7.

Senior management support was critical in the adoption and implementation of the technology. At the end of the purchasing phase, 60% of the senior managers were proponents, 30% were neutral, and 10% were resistant. As the graph depicts, once the information transformation had been underway (one to three years), the level of executive support jumped. After several years, 85% are proponents, 10% are neutral, and 5% are still resistant. The primary reason for this impressive jump in executive support is quite simple: strong evidence of payback. Once senior management witnessed the dramatic improvements in sales and critical performance measures such

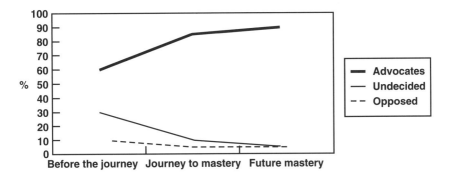

Figure 6.7   Evolution of executive support in retail

as expenses as a percentage of sales, they became information transformation zealots. When asked how the retailers viewed support in
the future for information transformation (over the next several
years), the executive support became 90%, with neutrals at 5% and
resisters at 5%.

Middle management level support in retail. While senior management were critical in the adoption and implementation of the technology, forward-thinking managers were important primarily during
implementation. As the graph shows, managers' support followed a
similar evolution to that of senior management.

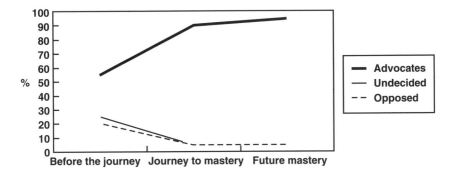

Figure 6.8   Evolution of management support in retail

Fifty five percent of managers were supporters in the early stages of
interest, which grew to 90% once the direct linkage to business
initiatives was established and evidence of payback was clear.

Managers became the most devoted group because of information business linkage and its ability to transform how the firm competed. The neutrals went from 25% to 5% after implementation. Retailers projected neutrals in the future at 5%. Resisters went from 20% to 5%. Comments were made that the neutrals and resisters had a lower likelihood of 'being around' in the future – a form of information-culture retirement.

General employee level support in retail. General employees were less involved until implementation but still as supportive as senior management and managers. Associates started out as 60% proponents and then evolved to 85% proponents as their involvement increased.

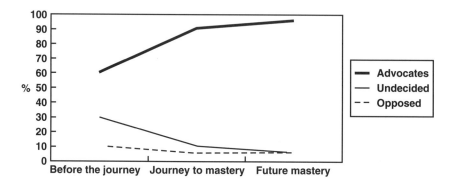

Figure 6.9   Evolution of general employee support in retail

This was due largely to the high productivity gains which information transformation provides, to the retailer's surprise: information transformation has given 100% productivity gains to many retailers. Resisters moved from 10% to 5%. The same sort of information culture retirement was in store for these resisters and neutrals as managers. This primarily is not a reduction in force, but the ones who resist change have found and will find an increasingly hostile environment.

Legacy of conflict between business and technology casts its shadow. In most of the firms there was tension between the business and technology organizations. Typical complaints from the business organization was that the technology organizations did not want to get sufficiently involved in the business needs and requirements of the information initiative. Typical complaints from the technology organizations were that the business organizations did not want to understand the inter-working of technology in order for business to do a better job at providing technology people with the information required for a successful implementation.

As a result, business began to believe that the technology organization was ineffective at addressing up-to-the-minute business conditions and market environments. This was devastating to the journey toward information mastery because even when the technological infrastructure was put in place, business did not believe in its capabilities. In the case of the technology organization, it was not a case of lack of competence. The technology group in many cases was trapped in the past of supporting legacy applications and did not have the resources to move into the future. As a result, their frequent answers were 'take a number'. Unfortunately, this fueled the perception of IT as ineffective.

This attitude became more deep-seated because the technology people could not do anything to counteract this endless cycle of being understaffed. There was a running joke that by the time you got back the information that you requested from the technology organization, you would have changed careers.

There were many amusing accounts of both the business and technology groups being brought into a meeting room to discuss the future implementation plans of the information initiative. One visionary equated this to a high school dance where the boys went to one side of the gym and the girls went to the other side of the gym – neither the boys nor girls wanted to talk to each other because of inherent discomfort.

In one case, a US retail executive mused that the entire information journey mirrored that of this high school dance scenario. Other stereotypes seem to be perpetuated by the inherent tension between the business and technology organizations, such as technology people being 'hippies' from the 1960s.

Lack of organizational harmony. The absence of collaboration between business and technology seemed to be the most damaging factor relative to organizational cooperation in the information initiative. Much of this stemmed from each group not wanting to enter the world of the other group. Business did not want to understand technology and technology did not want to understand business. This lack of cohesion cost many of the projects precious time and resources.

Comments made by business people were that the technology groups were more infatuated with the technology rather than wanting to really understand the potential value it could create. One visionary commented that the IT people just wanted to buy new toys for their sandbox.

Many of the firms felt that the information technology organizations were not a team player but in fact viewed the business organizations as a separate and distinct entity. As a result, the working relationship between business and technology never had a chance to become synergistic. This relationship paralleled that of a monopolistic relationship in the real world. One executive commented that: 'you just had to take what they dished out'.

One of the major problem areas in the interrelationship between business and technology organizations was the fact that there had been a historical precedent for the technology groups to promise business capabilities that never came to fruition. In this type of environment, no matter how good all the capabilities were, if the business people did not believe they would come true, they may as well not have existed.

> 'It got to the point where the technology group would tell us about a new future capability, we would just laugh to ourselves realizing that it would probably not come to pass.'

Under this scenario, the IT organizations were forever attempting to convince the business organizations that their capabilities did in fact exist while at the same time the business organizations were attempting to convince the technology groups that their view of the marketplace was correct.

All of these factors created an environment in which real progress between the two organizations was kept at bay.

Resistance to change. From the mass-market information legacies of the past, legacy attributes of the IT organization continued forward in time. In other words, the world had changed and the IT organization had not. One retail executive commented that: 'Our technology people have made some progress but not enough for us to be competitive in the marketplace and this has hurt us'.

Another US bank executive commented that: 'it would take a herd of elephants to pull their IT organization out of the past and into the 21st century'.

Another renegade commented that: 'the only way to create change within their IT organization was to remove the dead wood and replace it with fresh IT people from another industry altogether'.

The organizations that successfully transformed their technology function did so with strong involvement from senior management. In these cases, the senior management became directly involved with the visibility and culture of the technology organizations' involvement in these strategic initiatives and drove their acceptance. They also acted as the bridge between business and technology organizations in order to facilitate the mending of past wounds.

Adversary for information transformation. Most of the adversaries for information transformation battle the factions for positive change toward information mastery. The threat of this impending change had a high probability for creating impending doom for their position and power within the firm. These opponents of the information transformation typically were organizations that only existed because they had control over important aspects of acquiring and processing information within the firm. They had grown quite skilled over the years at developing information skills which increased their internal political power, as opposed to creating information skills which created additional customer and shareholder value. As a result, information was under their complete control, which created a restricted information flow throughout the firm.

One US retail executive stated that the organizations within his firm were: 'nothing but large information fortresses guarding the firm's most valuable resource from itself'.

Another US retailer commented that: 'the organizations that fared well under the past information environment were completely opposed to the new information transformation partly for political reasons'. This visionary also stated that: 'the road to 21st century information usage would totally disrupt the power they had created over years of doing things the old way'.

Many of these predispositions toward the new way of applying information existed because of the perception that the change was a negative event rather than a positive one. One US retail executive commented that: 'whole chunks of organizations would be gone under the new information environment, and they knew that'. As a result, these organizations did everything they could to forestall the new information environment.

One of the critical dynamics which occurred on the road to information mastery was the fact that early on in most of the information transformations, the early challenges of transformation created areas of vulnerability which served the adversaries of change quite well. One Australian banking executive commented that: 'the opponents of information change relished the fact that we were having great difficulties at the beginning of our initiative and took full advantage of it'.

Before most teams began their road to information transformation, they didn't realize how inextricably the firm's information was linked to factions of power within the firm. It became quite clear as the teams began to institute changes, which directly affected all aspects of an organization's ability and scope of decision-making.

One high street UK banking executive reflected on their early naivete: 'we soon realized that by changing the way organizations applied information, we were really fundamentally changing the power structure within the entire firm'.

Another UK banking executive commented that: 'for people who had spent their whole careers coveting information for political gain within the firm, the idea of relinquishing that power was very distasteful to say the least'.

The UK banking executive added that: 'had we known how difficult this task truly was when we had started, many of us would have thought twice about beginning this almost impossible task'.

One US investment banking executive commented on the decision framework within his firm:

> *'Decisions are driven by internal power, politics, and positioning.'*

One of the common problems which existed in most of the firms was that the firms had both field organizations and a central organization each of which wanted to determine the structure and use of the firm's collective information. This was a source of constant struggle in determining who would own the information. One visionary commented that his firm was made up of: 'autonomous field organizations with autonomous information making autonomous decisions'. The result was an operationally confused firm with confused customers.

One UK banking executive commented that his firm was run by: 'a group of autonomous field executives whose only goal was to drive their own organizations' success regardless of the cost to the entire organization's growth'. This attitude was the central inhibitor toward bringing into play the firm's entire information power in the broader context of their market.

This brings to light the central problem of moving a firm quickly along the road of information mastery – that human beings will act on what is best for them as they are not inherently altruistic. In other words, if there is no specific incentive in place for them to create value with their organizations' information beyond their organization, they will not apply the resources to do so.

Business and IT organizations in enabling technology procurement. Most firms brought to light interesting dynamics of interplay between business and IT organizations. In the beginning, initial interest in information transformation emanated from the business organization. In Figure 6.10, the beginning of the interest phase shows business involvement higher than IT (65% vs. 35% respectively).

As the business implications of information transformation became clearer and more accepted, the purchase process became more heavily weighted to IT involvement because of technical considerations (integration, sizing, etc.). Toward the end of the purchase process, the business/IT involvement was 45% vs. 55% respectively. As for total involvement and past and predicted future involvement, Figure 6.11 depicts the results.

The business and IT organizations had almost equal involvement (45% vs. 55% respectively) in the investment stage of information transformation. When asked which organization would drive the

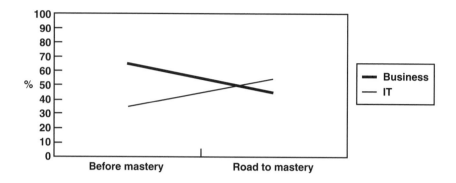

Figure 6.10   Business/IT involvement – investment process

expansion of the system, business was projected as the main driving force with respect to IT (90% vs. 10% respectively). This indicates the strong link of information transformation to business initiatives.

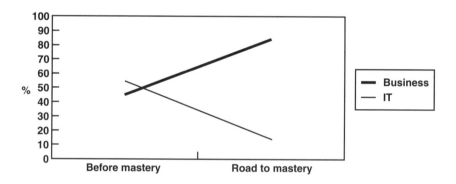

Figure 6.11   Business/IT involvement

Culture

Of all the aspects of transforming mass-market information legacies, the requirements of broad and deep corporate culture change were the most challenging.

The firms in the research addressed the cultural roadblocks to information mastery and the dynamics of cultural change from two perspectives. The first perspective addresses the cultural roadblocks themselves. The second perspective explores the issues surrounding the cultural change itself.

Culture can be defined as how the firm thinks about and subsequently approaches its business. Most firms in the research found that their approach was not aligned with the firm's culture. As a result, the information visionaries quickly found themselves amidst corporate chaos. The misalignment had a direct correlation to the bottom-line impact of the information transformation.

Much of the impact came through innovation. More specifically, transforming the information legacy requires an organization to think differently and think about different things. This type of thinking can be called 'Information Think'. It appeared throughout the research that most firms were not ready to 'think' about their business with the new atomic level of information. They were comfortable with summary information and high levels of uncertainty in business decisions, with what they did not know about their business. Also, the speed at which they transformed themselves was reflective of intrinsic issues of corporate culture. Such issues include:

✦ What is the speed and tenacity of transformation in the organization?
✦ Do the information visionaries have power and tenacity?
✦ Will the inherent culture doom information transformation prematurely?
✦ Is business and IT strategically and informationally aligned?

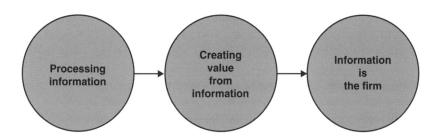

Figure 6.12   The customer information culture continuum

The perception legacy

Most of the firms found that the legacy of how people perceive the relevance of customer information to their jobs was a daunting task to change. Many employees still felt that customer information was only one tool of their job, rather than the primary competency by which they completed most activities within their job.

Another challenge which arose consistently was that people felt that customer information which was created by technology detracted from their contribution to any particular decision in which the information from technology was applied. People want to believe that it is their inherent intelligence that determines a good or bad decision in the business environment. Therefore it is hard for them to attribute a good or bad decision to information which was derived using technology rather than their own inherent intelligence.

One visionary commented that: 'people had a hard time giving credit to the information environment because they felt somehow that giving credit could detract from their worth as a person in the firm'. Conversely, if the decision was a bad decision, the information environment was the first to be blamed.

It was also very evident that regardless of how robust the customer information environment was people still had a bias toward decisions that perpetuated their historical approaches to business. They also had decision biases toward projects to which they had emotional ties. These types of biases kept them from fully gaining the true potential of a robust information environment.

Human beings also have a tendency to determine a course of action prior to receiving the supporting information. In this case, they have the propensity to frame the problem in the context of their predetermined answer. Human beings also will bias their decisions based on their predisposition toward the perceived inherent risk of the decision rather than accurate information generated in a strong information environment.

All of these human biases hold the firm back from achieving the full value of its information.

As one information visionary stated: 'you could have the most brilliant information environment in the world and if your people don't believe it will help them, they will never use it'.

This is the heart of the information master's success.

Transformation through learning

In the beginning, most firms entered the brave new world of customer information mastery with enthusiasm and hope. They began the process of learning with the hypothesis that operating the business at a higher level of information detail would have an impact on the bottom line. Through the elation and excitement came reality – applying detailed customer information is difficult.

More firms were not used to thinking along the lines of – What is it that I do not know which is most important to my customers? Then came the realization that the area initially scoped for the customer information transformation may not be the best use of their resources. This realization was and is most likely unavoidable when trying to apply a new level of customer detail to the business.

There is also the dilemma of re-prioritizing resources and making the humbling acknowledgement that a different path than the one originally chosen may make more long-term business sense. Both the old and the new paths are dimly lit and equally uncharted, but now they have some navigating experience and their senses tell them that the probability of payback will be higher down this new path. They travel for a while, burying the dead and carrying the wounded, knowing that their gut still says the payback warrants the perseverance.

This gut feeling emanates from two sources:

1 The visionaries have a personal vision of how their firm will be able to fundamentally change how they apply customer information in the pursuit of revenue.

2 The visionaries suspect that their competitors are furiously going down the same path and may have already made significant strides in customer and operational information, substantially lowering expense as a percentage of sales ratio.

Customer information legacy subcultures

There were common customer information legacy subcultures, which appeared to permeate the overall culture of mass markets. Eight main information legacy subcultures were identified in the research:

+ product vs. customer view;
+ all customers are equal;
+ legacy definitions of the desirability of customer activities;
+ legacy profitability;
+ measuring the past vs. servicing the future;
+ administer the firm's information vs. generate value;
+ group-think vs. innovation.

Product vs. customer view

The biggest challenges for firms on the road to customer information mastery is the shift from a product-oriented culture to a customer-oriented culture. Until the firm makes the shift to a customer-oriented culture, the most brilliant information capabilities will lie dormant. Many firms experienced this scenario first hand after they had implemented the first phase of information transformation. The employees had the ability to access tremendous customer-oriented information yet they were still attempting to apply product-oriented information because that is how they had historically approached their marketplace.

+ How many existing products did we sell?
+ How many new products did we sell?
+ What was the average volume of a certain product category?

The customer information masters understood that information is only as good as the culture in which it is applied.

All customers are equal

Another inherent problem, which was widespread within most of the firms, is that regardless of how well their information could potentially differentiate customers, unless the employees believed that customers were different, the information that differentiated these customers was relatively useless. One information UK banking executive commented that: 'for so long our firm has treated all customers the same; it is part of our culture to continue to do so even though our information shows us how vast the difference in customer behavior and profitability really is'.

The UK banking executive continues: 'if we collectively believe they are not different, no amount of information in the world will ever change that culture unless we drive that change ourselves'.

Legacy definitions of the desirability of customer activities

Another problem which seemed to tax most firms' ability to derive the maximum value from their information was the fact that the firm's definition of good and bad customer activities remained linked to definitions of legacy market conditions. The most prevalent example in this area was where firms previously would avoid high-risk business ventures because they did not have the appropriate level of information to price correctly for that level of risk; they avoided those particular business ventures. As firms improved their level of information relative to the attributes of risk in particular business ventures, they found themselves still tied to the old way of pricing risk because the definitions of good and bad business ventures had not changed in their mind, regardless of new information which was now available to them.

One of the UK banking executives stated: 'although our goal was now to say that there was no such thing as a good or bad business venture, just a good or bad price for that business venture, we were still trapped by the past in thinking that all risky business was bad'.

Legacy profitability

Legacy profitability had a tremendous impact on a firm's ability to move quickly toward the objective of information mastery. In most cases, this condition of current profitability was the result of actions taken in the past under legacy market conditions. This created a tremendous complacency within the firm when it came to making significant changes in almost any competency. One US banking executive commented as to his firm's attitude: 'why should we change, we made a lot of money this year and I still received a paycheck'.

Unfortunately, the real driver for change is usually some type of financial or operational disaster in the firm. Many of the firms reported that significant progress was made on the road to information mastery only when the journey was preceded by conditions within the firm that were perceived as being a corporate tragedy.

Measuring the past vs. servicing the future

Many firms struggled with the cultural issues of measuring past performance vs. changing for the future. This particular predisposition had a significant impact on the degree and quickness of change relative to information transformation. Many firms were still mired in looking at their past performance rather than a view toward serving the future needs of customers and shareholders. In many cases, the firm's view of the value of their information was predominantly to support the viewing of past financial and operational performance such as a profit and loss statement. One litmus test for a firm's information culture is to measure what percentage of time is spent by senior executives discussing past performance of the profit and loss statement vs. future innovations to create value for customers.

In part this cultural transformation entails bringing in new people from different industries. One Australian banking executive comments: 'We have never been a marketing-oriented firm so we really need to buy new talent from industries that have been market oriented'.

Administer the firm's information vs. generate value

A firm's ability to exploit its information is as much to do with its attitude toward the role information plays within the firm. In most cases, the majority of a firm's resources are geared toward administering or managing information rather than to creating or generating value for customers and shareholders. In other words, information is seen as a processing necessity rather than the source for a firm's differentiation in the marketplace. One visionary states that: 'after we are done processing the information to get our account statements out to the customers, we view it as having little use'. Also, many firms still view information as an expense or an overhead item rather than a core asset.

Group-think vs. innovation

Another inhibitor for progress on the road to information mastery is the propensity for a firm to be engulfed in group-think vs. exploiting the innovation or business options that a rich information environment can yield. In many cases, the firms were so engulfed in restrictive corporate cultures that brilliant business opportunities which were made known from a rich information environment could not be pursued because the firm was constricted by its own complex and conservative nature. This is particularly true in certain geographies around the world because of inherent regional cultures.

This UK banking visionary elaborated by saying that: 'firms that are driven by compromise are constrained to compromised innovation'.

Customer cultural transformation

The successful transformation of a firm's customer culture is the essence of what the information masters have come to understand. It is probably one of the most difficult challenges a firm will ever face. The firm's culture holds its legacies of the past and its opportunities for the future.

Most firms who achieved a powerful corporate culture did so under the following three conditions:

1   It was part of their genetic makeup from the start.
2   They experienced a catastrophic corporate event.
3   They employed powerful and visionary senior executives.

Other than these three conditions, human nature tended to hold the firm back to the unknowns of its business history. It is also because of human nature that firms lean toward changing the things within the firm which are inherently easier to change. Physical things within a firm, such as buildings, furnishings, and even technology, are more attractive in terms of their inherent ability to change. It is people's nature to look away from the more difficult issues of changing the way employees think about their jobs, their company, and the future.

As the firm continues to change the easier things about itself and further looks away from the more difficult aspects of change the likelihood to change becomes less. As the firm continues further down this path without systemic change, the severity of the required antidote becomes more severe.

All the while, the adversaries for change lie in wait for any mistakes or aberrations from the path of corporate correctness.

One US telecommunications visionary described how his firm started their initiative toward long-term change. They first started their project as a very low profile information project. They carefully measured the small winds which occurred within the information project. They then gradually increased the profile of the information project within the firm to gradually socialize the benefits that the firm would receive from this project implemented on a broader scale.

This strategy worked well for this particular project which was being implemented in a larger firm. Smaller firms have less of a cultural challenge than larger firms. This is true because of two factors – complexity and inertia.

One US retailing visionary commented on the difficulties of a large firm moving through long-term change: 'our biggest challenge will be to sustain our people's willingness to fight the incredibly difficult times ahead of us on this path to significant change'.

Achieving systemic transformation

As discussed earlier, many of the firms that did not have the type of culture which facilitated change ended up experiencing systemic change after catastrophic events. One UK banking visionary commented on the impetus for his firm to experience the beginnings of systemic cultural change: 'our firm took a huge hit in profitability last year which really woke everyone up, and that's what has created the climate for change'. He added that 'the only concern he has beyond this series of events is the question of what level of catastrophe will be required to drive the next set of changes in culture'.

One of the critical elements to not only start cultural change but to sustain it is the socialization of the benefits of change. Many firms found that after they started small information mastery projects, and began the process of communicating the benefits of those projects within the firm, receptivity to change increased. One visionary commented that: 'it was incredible to see how people's attitude towards change evolved once they saw that the change could positively affect what they did and how they did it'.

Most of the firms found it helpful to start in a small area in order to prove a concept would benefit the firm from that small area of success. It is only human nature that large initiatives draw more human attention within a firm. Small projects are more likely to be left alone initially because they tend to be perceived as more innocuous. This gives the time for the wheels of success to start turning.

As one US telecommunications visionary commented: 'we were just the small little project tucked away in a quarter of our corporation when we first began and that was fine with us'.

In the reality of corporate initiatives, if the project never gets to mature within the firm, they may as well not have started the project. Another challenge is that even if the project is small and well hidden within the firm, and the firm does not ultimately believe in the viability of the project, it is doomed to failure.

Firms found that a systematic approach to breaking down the adversaries for cultural change was effective. This usually entailed the support of senior management and other key mid-level management. One US retailing visionary commented: 'The more barriers to change we broke down, the easier the next barriers were to topple'.

Culture is the heart of competency

Most firms found that at the heart of their customer information competency was the customer culture. One US retailing visionary observed that: 'if you look around at all the very successful companies who have made their mark in an industry, their distinguishing factor is that of culture'.

It is firms who give a high profile to their people who drive change, innovation, and new ways of doing things that ultimately will be the first to change the rules by which their industry operates.

It is these firms who are the first to change the rules in their industry that will capture the best markets and customers within that industry.

The main problem that hounds the firms is self-induced. They do not plan or commit resources to the necessary change in culture. It is assumed that the culture will transform itself naturally. But as we have seen, this only happens when the firm experiences dire financial conditions.

The retailers with intensive customer focus exhibited superior information transformation. One retailer overtly drove information culture change as a corporate edict.

Leadership

In general, executive leadership in customer information competency was lacking perhaps more than any other category. This is not necessarily a commentary on the current batch of senior management but more a comment on the lack of deep and strategic understanding of the role information plays in the future of any consumer-intensive firm.

The customer information visionary

One of the most crucial elements of the firms who were on the road to information mastery was the existence of an individual who represented the heartbeat of the firm's customer information – the information visionary. This individual represented a multiplicity of roles within the firm: information visionary, whipping post, corporate hero, chief troublemaker, change agent, and master salesman.

It was very interesting to observe that these information visionaries were perhaps the most crucial individuals relative to the firm's ability to transform their information competency; yet these individuals who performed these roles within most of the firms did so at great risk to their careers. In essence, these individuals or corporate information visionaries represented the end to business as usual and the beginning of the art of all future possibilities for the firm.

The CIO (Chief Information Officer) is not, by default, the firm's information visionary. This is a common misconception. Certain CIOs merely function in an administrative capacity, while others are the true change agents with a visionary goal for their firm's customer information competency.

These information visionaries not only created the spark for information transformation but also fanned the flame for continuous change. In almost every single firm, there was one person who could be singled out as the information visionary. This individual was usually the person who provided the link between middle management and senior management in order to facilitate change at multiple levels within the firm. This individual also could be characterized as a person who had the genetics to suit this very tumultuous role. In other words, the personality characteristics of such an individual were hard coded from birth and not developed as traditional corporate skills. This one person is typically the epicenter of informational change, one of the most important ingredients for transformation from the legacy.

In the ideal circumstance, the visionary has presence in both the business and technology side of the business. This visionary, in many cases, must be in a 'bet the farm' environment because of the political and power implications of information transformation.

The visionaries carry much of the burden for change. They are the primary catalysts for the cultural change as well.

Function of the information visionary

The essence of the visionary is to move the business down the road to information mastery as quickly and consistently as possible. The visionary must balance the sometimes conflicting short-term and long-term objectives of the supporters while working off continuous attacks from the adversaries of change. The visionary must always have one foot in reality while at the same time keeping one foot firmly planted in the future vision of information possibilities. The visionary must have the realism of a project manager to keep change alive while painting an information vision of doing business in new ways and at new levels.

The information visionary's function can be summed up as:

✦ skilled seller of vision;
✦ supreme marketing guru;
✦ clandestine technical wizard;
✦ would-be statistician;

- ✦ master of the carnival;
- ✦ street gang leader;
- ✦ business-as-usual traitor;
- ✦ working juggler;
- ✦ gifted plotter.

In the research, when examining the firms who experienced low payback, several of the visionaries were or had become dysfunctional. In several situations, the visionary was present at the beginning and either left for another position or reduced their level of involvement in the project. One retail senior vice president commented that it took them an additional year to achieve the payback because he had reduced his personal involvement. He had set up the teams and visionary disciples to carry on the work. He then shifted his attentions to other areas, and soon after that the information transformation lost momentum and energy. He finally re-engaged himself and moved on with the information transformation.

One firm's information visionary had very little political power. She was at a lower level in the organization and did not have the necessary clout to drive the required change. The visionary fought fiercely but ended up discouraged and burned out from the constant uphill battle, and ultimately left the organization. At the same time, there was a person who claimed to be the information visionary and was not. This self-proclaimed information visionary was in a position of power yet really did not have an information vision for the firm nor was he engaged in the transformation process. Both conditions were deadly to payback.

One observation is that the true visionary is rarely self-proclaiming, unlike the false information visionary. The true visionary regularly earned badges of courage as a result of being at the heart of the storm. This visionary was what each business publicly stated they needed but privately ended by crucifying because of the turmoil. The factions in the business who were well rewarded by the status quo feared the information visionary and relentlessly attacked the change efforts. The information visionary was often the embodiment of change – change that would usually redefine and redistribute power.

The information visionary defined the foundation and pace of information transformation. In each business, the visionary was the individual who prophesied to senior management and decision-makers the potential value of the information transformation relative to their investment in time and resources.

The successful information visionary was tenacious about evangelizing the message with zeal and enthusiasm. This role was most often a make or break condition of a successful transformation.

In cases where there was an effective information visionary, the correlation to the size of impact was overwhelming.

In those businesses where the information visionary did not have individual political power, but still was successful, they were tied to a powerful executive who supported his or her actions.

In healthy environments, the visionaries were allowed to fail. One executive commented: 'We decided to give them a little room to succeed without the fear of failure'.

Personality traits of the information visionary

The information visionary had very specific traits that seemed to be consistent in most of the successful information visionaries. As stated earlier, these traits were not traits developed through many years of corporate life but in fact were fundamental personality traits from birth.

If a firm work to create the perfect information visionary with the best traits from the best visionary, that individual would be described as:

+ bright and imaginative;
+ rebel sage;
+ at ease with statistics;
+ gambler;
+ divergent nature;
+ dogged and impatient about implementing;
+ magnetic;
+ storyteller.

Bright and imaginative

This individual must be bright and imaginative in order to succeed with the tremendous challenges which lie ahead on the road to information mastery. It will take every bit of intelligence and imagination to ferret out the perils of the corporate legacy. They must be proactive in their bids to change areas of the business, which will give them the foothold to move forward to the more difficult areas of change.

Rebel sage

This person must be a rebel sage. It is not enough to have business savvy or be technologically aware. This person must have a clear vision for information and the strategic application of the information across business units. They must hold this vision clear but stay realistic about providing particular short-term wins with their information transformation. Most firms in the research had at least one information visionary who had sufficient vision. Even so, the visionary must transfer this vision to the people employed in the effort as well as to senior executives. This was extremely difficult because most executives are tied to very concrete, short-term objectives and major information transformation is long term in nature. Most of the information visionaries were able to secure short-term objectives, which satisfied at least a minimum of the senior management team. In many cases, visionaries were forced to focus on short-term results, relinquishing a focus on long-term transformation and ultimately larger benefits to the firm.

At ease with statistics

The information visionary does not have to be a statistician, but should be comfortable with the conceptual application of mathematics to sophisticated information applications. In complex business environments, an understanding of mathematics is essential to create value from the information. In essence, advanced mathematics is the only way to handle or address the complexity of the available information.

Gambler

The visionary must be comfortable with taking risks because most of the information activities are high-risk. In order to drive higher overall value for the firm, the visionary must execute transformation activities, which threaten powerful positions within the firm. Most of the information visionaries were comfortable with these types of risks. The visionary must also be ready to break corporate rules because most of the existing rules were set up for the business environments of 20 years ago. The rules were set up for the efficient processing of information and not to create value from the information for customers and shareholders simultaneously.

Divergent nature

The visionary must have a divergent nature, as much of his or her activities will be contrary to business as usual; most of the visionaries in the research were. Much of this discussion is not about a type of corporately nurtured behavior but about the inherent nature of the individual. The 'mold' of an information visionary is more about genetics than it is about corporately developed business skills.

Dogged and impatient about implementing

Doggedness is probably one of the most important attributes a visionary can possess. Most of the visionaries observed in the research were utterly exhausted from their transformation efforts. Nonetheless, most of them had a relentless desire to move their information initiative forward and were willing to somehow surmount any obstacles.

Magnetic

The most successful visionaries had magnetic personalities. This was very important in persuading people to change, and in acquiring the best people to work on the initiative. It is also essential in gaining the maximum executive support or dealing with any hostile actions within the business with a degree of flair and likeability. In several cases, projects came very close to failure because of the visionary's lack in ability to persuade or sell the idea even though the project had specific successes.

Storyteller

Much of what the visionary does is telling the story of a vision of an information transformation as well as short-term wins. Many visionaries found the task of operationalizing the projects required so much of their efforts that communications suffered. In several cases, the visionaries hired specific communications people to support this role. In one specific case, a separate person was hired to facilitate communications between the business units.

Optimum conditions for the visionary

There were very specific conditions where visionaries fared better than others. Very rarely were they the top executives. Positions ranged from project manager status to occasionally senior vice presidential level. Some of the optimum conditions are as follows:

+ timing for sufficient political power;
+ timing of higher organizational awareness of importance of information;
+ competitive pressures at all time high;
+ recent moves by competitors to invest in information;
+ opportunity to sustain information efforts beyond short-term initiative.

Timing for sufficient political power

The visionary must wield sufficient political power at the proper time in order to succeed. If the visionary is reliant on a sponsoring executive's power, the timing of that executive's power is critical. In one particular firm there was a high-level executive who understood that the firm needed to bring their information legacy into the 21st century. He attempted to put the right resources in place during a time where the central group of the firm had low political power in relation to the different geographical business units. When the project was implemented, the project required close cooperation, and sharing of information to create the maximum value for the firm. Because central political power was low, the business units could easily avoid supplying information even though it was for the good of the whole organization. The visionary's position was weakened by the failure of the business units to cooperate, and he ultimately resigned from the firm. This visionary person was no less visionary now than he was when he started the initiative but simply timed his transformation efforts during a period when his political power was not at its height.

In many cases, the political support lasted a certain period of time. One Northern European banking visionary commented on his executive sponsor:

> 'No, not sugar daddies . . . godfathers. Sugar daddies will forgive you. Godfathers will kill you. I have to get there (be successful) within two years. Because one day they will ask the question, and they want to hear positive results.'

Timing of organizational awareness

The timing of the organization's awareness is critically important for understanding the value of information as well as the value of the ability to apply that information. A firm that values information and its ability to apply it does not necessarily guarantee the success of a large information project. Many times a firm has a high perceived value on information and its ability to apply it yet they have defined information and their ability incorrectly.

One particular firm in the research had such a problem. There was tremendous corporate visibility for increasing the firm's ability to apply information, complete with numerous seminars on information and various aspects of data mining. Most of these activities were surface events that did not initiate concrete actions or steps of transformation. They conducted many seminars and internal meetings about information and their ability to apply it. Many of the seminars were titled 'data mining' even though the firm was far from being close to implementing such advanced applications of information.

There was no true information visionary to drive their collective vision and change the firm. There were many interested parties and smart people beginning to think about the information initiatives and concepts yet no collective momentum. There was a rather heated discussion at board level, about information competency for this particular firm, with the head of retail financial services. A very senior executive absolutely rejected the fact that his firm had a problem with customer information and profitability. The same discussions had taken place with people several levels down from the executive boards, but they realized the severity of the problem.

In many of the firms that were undergoing their information initiatives, the visionary had a much easier time when there had been some very obvious aggressive moves by a known competitor in the same market. In one firm, the business had undergone its first major loss in several hundred years. This provided the perfect environment for the visionary to work through difficult changes. Even so, the changes the visionary was able to effect were only within his particular business unit.

The information visionary's existence was clearly bipolar. This individual created supporters and enemies in just about all groups and organizations within the firm. As a result, the perception of this individual embodied the full range of symbols:

✦ corporate savior/scoundrel;
✦ foe/ally of technology groups;
✦ foe/ally of business groups;
✦ liberator/demolisher of the firm.

The roles for the information visionary tended to be different depending on whether the visionary resided on the business or IT organization. In many cases, if the information visionary were on the business side, one of the major challenges would be to have the technology people understand the informational needs from a business perspective. If the information visionary were on the technology side, one of the major challenges would be to give the business a basic understanding of the enabling technology and how information could best be used to support the business.

One of the sensitivities for the information visionary from the IT side was that if the renegade was successful, they would produce an information environment that would be much more independent of IT. In other words, the business people could execute traditional IT initiatives on their own without picking up the phone to call the technology people for assistance. This was a threat to the technology people in many cases. One US retailing visionary commented: 'if we wanted to make adjustments to our reporting in any one of our databases we had to wait until our IT group got around to making them, which usually was too long for us'.

In one major US retailer, a similar situation arose where an information environment was created for the buying function of a major retailer where buyers would find quick answers to very complex questions. Finding answers to these questions traditionally required dedicated resources from the IT organization. As one retail executive commented: 'once we had the information capabilities we didn't have to call our technology group anymore and could do most of the traditionally technological activities by ourselves'.

The wannabe visionary

In many of the firms there existed information visionaries that were only wannabe information visionaries. These individuals did not have the characteristics or the nature necessary to drive the type of change required to navigate the road to information mastery. These types of individuals were extremely dangerous to the cultural health of a firm about to embark on a very perilous journey. Many times these individuals would dub themselves the information visionary for purely self-serving reasons within the firm. One true Australian banking visionary discussed their perception of a wannabe visionary in their firm: 'they knew this whole information thing was starting to get a very high profile within the firm but really didn't know what to do with it'.

Another true Australian visionary commented on their wannabe visionary: 'they made sure that they were all at the high-profile corporate meetings using all the buzz words about data warehouse, data mining, and data marts but really didn't know what they were talking about'.

One particular Australian bank had a very high profile wannabe visionary who was convincing people that the firm was headed in the right direction and was making good progress on the road to information mastery. In reality, most of the activities were tactical and short-lived with little real systemic change occurring. This wannabe visionary wielded a great deal of political power but did not have sufficient vision and courage to drive the firm forward into the future.

The actual information visionary happened to be in a position of insufficient political power to affect sufficient change within the organization. It was this visionary that was actually generating the vision for the entire firm relative to their information mastery. The real Australian banking visionary commented that: 'the vision was coming from levels which did not get the airplay they needed to really capture the firm's attention and ultimately our transformation failed'.

Ultimately, the firm's efforts to transform their information competency failed in the broader scheme of their information efforts. The real information visionary ended up losing the stamina to continue and left the firm.

These wannabe visionaries created a very dangerous condition for those true visionaries who aspired to conquer their information legacy. These false visionaries also created a false sense of momentum or security for the business that thought they were progressing. It was not always the case that the pseudo visionary was self-proclaiming. Many times certain powerful people within the firm would falsely dub someone their firm's information visionary. This happened because these powerful people didn't understand the role of a true information visionary. The person whose title was chief information officer or vice president of information technology was often tagged with the information visionary title.

In one high street UK bank, there was a very well publicized, charismatic vice president of information technology who carried this perceived distinction. In actuality, this person was very well presented in public and the press but did not understand how to sufficiently transform this large firm's information competency into 21st century terms. As a result, their progress has been anemic. The real information visionary was at a much lower level in the organization. A clever top executive who supported the true information visionary quietly managed the change capabilities of the organization by only making known what information transformation he felt the organization could psychologically handle. The majority of the information activity remained underneath the corporate radar. As a result, strong progress was made in his 'skunk works' area.

In one large US telecommunications firm, one of the information visionaries was very dedicated to his efforts to evolve his firm's information legacy. In many discussions he had with his peers, he realized that they didn't understand what he was trying to do with his information vision. He decided the best thing for him in moving forward was to keep his work relatively quiet. He commented that the best thing that could happen was that his peers would leave him to 'skunk works' information initiatives. This was often the situation because many information visionaries were in a particular group with specific objectives. As a result, it was more effective for them to accomplish their objectives underneath the corporate radar.

This condition was more dangerous than a visionary who was in a position of low political power. In the case where a pseudo-visionary and real visionary existed simultaneously, the pseudo-visionary often endangered the potential impact of the real information visionary. What makes this situation very dangerous is that if a firm misunderstands what would be the correct information vision for that firm, they will misunderstand the role of the information visionary.

In one Australian bank, there was a lower level information visionary who worked extremely hard to change the marketing practices of the firm. Another person in the firm was regarded by the general populace to be the official information visionary. This person knew that new ways of applying information had value but didn't know how to go about evolving their information legacy. As a result, the attention, focus, and resources were addressed to this pseudo-information visionary. As a result, the resources were misdirected.

In many of the businesses, the pseudo-information visionary would be used as a platform for political advancement, gain the attention of executives and move forward with symbolic and self-serving activities that had little to do with conquering the information problems facing the firm.

The perils of being an information visionary

There are inherent risks in being a visionary. By definition the visionary has to operate outside the bounds of the business's traditions. As a result, they are subject to corporate ostracism and consternation. They represent change and therefore they are the enemy. They are also an easy target of the enemies of information mastery because the results of information initiatives are many times difficult to measure and easy to dispute.

There are many perils involved in being an information visionary. In most instances, the visionary is forced to operate at the fringes of what the firm deems, as being acceptable practices. By default this behavior draws unending criticism and ridicule from those in traditional groups within the firm. In other words, the information visionary represents the possible demise of tradition – tradition which has served the factions of the status quo quite well. In addition, the work of the information visionary is very difficult to quantify and prove in many of the areas of systemic change. As a result, it is difficult to support benefits by hard facts as much of the change takes place over an extended period of time. It is then critical that their efforts be sheltered from the continuous barrage of attacks from adversaries. This form of protection usually must emanate from the highest levels within the firm. Without this shelter given by senior executives, the information visionary and the transformation is in grave danger of being swept away along with many other initiatives.

A small proportion of these people fell victim to factions of complacency within the firm and these careers were damaged in the short term. An equally small number of visionaries became internal stars. Many times they moved out of the firm and into consulting activities. The inherent challenge of the visionary is long term in nature. Today's long-term projects are the most susceptible to short-term corporate winds.

Barricade or change agent

The role of the executives was critically important. Of all factors studied, executive sponsorship was the most commonly cited factor which influenced the outcome of the information transformation.

Senior management and its role in information mastery ranged anywhere from being a barricade to the central change agent. Unfortunately, more of the senior management were identified as being a barricade to this road of mastery than were facilitators toward information mastery. This did change over time as senior management saw the acceptance and benefit that was being created from this information competency and felt that it was in their own best interest to become involved in such an initiative.

Regrettably, the senior management that were adversaries of information mastery could many times do more damage than the advocates of information mastery. One member of a senior UK banking management team was infamous for stating that: 'I have never let a lack of information interfere with my ability to make decisions'.

In several cases, it was clear that the major inhibitor for change was not one or two members of the senior management team but in fact the chief executive officer. One high street UK banking visionary commented that the most important change that could be made to bring their firm competitively into the next century was a change in the CEO.

It was evident that change could occur more quickly in the lower levels of the organization than in the upper reaches of senior management. One US retail visionary commented: 'The further you go up into our organization the less likely change will occur'.

Interviewing the success factors for many of the firms who chose to move down the road for information mastery, the issues of senior management support plagued most of them. It is important to look at the essence of why the lack of senior management support was so prevalent. Much had to do with the fact that senior management was incentivized to achieve short-term results which placed the priority of long-term systemic change low on the priority list. One US banking visionary commented: 'unless you get at least one strong faction of senior management behind information mastery initiatives, the challenges are likely to be insurmountable'.

This US banking visionary added that: 'Our strategic direction is short-term results'.

For the senior management which really took the time to illustrate the importance of information and its application to the future of the firm, the results were significant. In many firms where there was significant senior management support, attitudes consistently changed toward information competency. One of the US retailing information visionaries commented on such a senior executive who became actively involved in the change: 'we had a member of the senior management team actually get involved to send a clear message that information was this firm's most powerful weapon and most valuable asset'.

Tackling the strategic role of customer information

One of the most difficult issues to address within the firms who attempted customer information mastery was dealing with a question of information and its strategic role within the firm. For a century firms have dealt with information as an administrative requirement for the successful operation of the firm. Now the visionaries are asking the same firm to make a radical change in how the firm as a whole views and addresses the strategic value and implications of the firm's information. This issue of viewing information differently from a strategic perspective is probably one of the most difficult things to change in the short term. In addition, the tactical information initiatives where employees use the latest buzzwords play havoc with perceptions of real systemic change.

One US banking visionary commented on their firm's lack of a strategic information direction: 'our executives really haven't come to grips with what information is to this firm'.

The issue of information and its role in the future of a firm must be addressed at all levels of the organization. It is important to continually focus on the value that can be created both for customers and for shareholders when trying to understand the strategic implications of information competency. One of the most daunting challenges facing any firm is addressing the issue of the decentralization and how the value of information across business units can be applied for maximum synergy and value. One UK banking visionary comments: 'We have a bunch of different business units with their own separate information systems that produce little or no value in terms of raising the overall opportunity for cross-business-unit value'.

The persistence of mistrust

The persistence of mistrust between senior management and middle management in the context of submitting initiatives for corporate approval and funding was prevalent in the areas of information competency. This mistrust had been cultivated over generations of management as an accepted norm of behavior. It was spelled out in the unwritten laws of middle management that in order to get approval for any initiative, the projected payback needed to be accentuated. This created the historical belief that most projected payback projections from most initiatives would be automatically escalated. This caused senior management to automatically distrust and discount the projected numbers of payback from initiatives such as information-related initiatives. These mechanics of proposing projects created an escalating projection of payback cycle where the senior management continued to require larger payback numbers because of their knowledge that most payback estimates were inflated and in turn middle management continued to escalate their projected payback numbers in response to senior management's reaction. This vicious cycle was one of the central challenges in actually obtaining sponsorship and funding to begin some of the early information mastery initiatives.

Retail is detail

There is an expression which retailers are very fond of stating – 'Retail is Detail', or 'The dollars lie in the details'. This statement is something that the information masters understand intuitively. This statement is something that the firms who are on the road to mastery are beginning to appreciate as they move further and further through their journey towards information competency. Much of this appreciation has to do with the growing understanding that there is tremendous value in resolving uncertainty in the business environment and the value that resolving this uncertainty brings to the business.

The essence of information competency is a firm's ability to determine which of the things it does not know that would have the highest value if it knew. This concept is the central aspect of regaining a working intimacy with the business and its customers. If we looked at human beings and how they have evolved over the years, little substantive change has taken place. The corollary in the business world is that customer buying behavior has changed little as well. The fact that firms have grown further away from the intimacy of the quaint corner drugstore has to do with the explosion of scale and complexity of the business environment rather than a perception that human behavior has fundamentally changed. In fact, businesses have washed away this once intimate knowledge of their customers by aggregating their views of customers because of the scale of today's business.

Business has only recently begun to take the shroud off of customer intimacy by employing technological advances in storing and analyzing massive amounts of detailed information. These technological advances have enabled firms to start making systemic changes in all aspects of the firm's ability to apply customer, operational and financial information more effectively and efficiently.

Information and its availability have a profound effect on people's behavior. As in most firms, the people who interact with customers would use better information if it were readily available to them. As a result, customers would have a better chance of being satisfied. This is the case with almost any function within a firm.

Information has a tremendous power to guide actions both for employees and for customers. It can lead an employee to service a customer in a particular way as well as lead a customer to behave in a more profitable way. This can be accomplished by not only giving information to the employee or customer that will lead them to a certain behavior but also to measure the outcome of that particular behavior.

In many cases, when firms demand those employees be customer focused, they neglect to give the employees adequate information in order to execute that demand. As a result when the employee attempts to comply with that request, the employee gets frustrated and the customer service level falls short. As human beings, the path of the least resistance is initially the most desirable. If firms were to use information to lead employees down the path of least resistance in the way they service customers, two objectives could be accomplished simultaneously. The employee could gain job satisfaction by having the information available which would ultimately satisfy the customer and the customer would be satisfied because the employee has the information he or she needed to respond to the customer's needs.

As part of this information-guided action for employees, information's role as a measurement tool is widely misused. In many cases, firms set up measurements of performance which fall short of actually capturing the essence of what the form is trying to achieve. It is widely known that in the telecommunications industry, there is a high degree of churning of customers from one product offering to the next. Many times, the salespeople will be paid new customer acquisition bonuses for customers who are not actually new customers but merely just churning back and forth between product offerings.

Another misuse of information as a measurement tool is in the short-term orientation of measurement rather than the long-term orientation of measurement. In most consumer-intensive industries, there is an abuse, which occurs because salespeople are rewarded for acquiring new customers but not to compensate for the length of time they continue to be a customer. One visionary comments that: 'Our sales teams know that they can acquire a massive amount of customers without worrying about whether they even stay more than a month because they are not penalized for customer tenure'.

Another US banking visionary comments that: 'we love to show our high profile measures of success, yet underneath it all, we are not really sure whether we have fundamentally moved the business forward'.

As a result, information as a measurement device is suspect in many business environments today.

The information masters' approach is to put in place specific processes which are led by iterative information flows which carefully lead employees through the process of predicting and understanding customer behavior and needs. As a customer reacts to this iterative process, there are mechanisms in place to iterate on how the employee is guided through this information-based process relative to specific customer reactions. This is the essence of information mastery – to have well-defined understanding of customer needs and behaviors, to have the information at the point of contact, and to have it in an iterative process, which changes depending on customer response.

As one Australian banking visionary stated: 'for our firm to really interact with customers and at the same time have our collective knowledge grow based on those reactions has been a radical change for us'.

Information as a strategy

Most firms had some semblance of an information strategy. Most of the information strategies contained the right words but lacked the vision and implementation to make them a reality. Most of the strategies revolved around technological-oriented competencies with some consideration toward operational implementation. Because most of the information strategies were directed at central information views, the reality of a diverse and distributed business unit structure made them almost impossible to implement.

Information has historically been relegated to the confines of the technology organization and has not been fully implemented as a strategic asset. As a result, the vast majority of resources surrounding the exploitation of a firm's information is largely administration rather than value creation. This perpetuates the huge void between what is stated as a firm's strategy and what has really been implemented as well as taken to heart by the firm.

Administrative vs. customer information

One litmus test as to where a firm was on the road to information mastery was the balance of its resources dedicated toward either administrative uses of information relative to resources dedicated toward customer-oriented uses of information. It was evident after you scratched below the surface of slogans and high profile business initiatives that the majority of firms' resources were still targeted toward the routine processing of transactional and administrative details of business operations.

For the information master, the balance toward customer-related information activities far outweighed the traditional transactional and administrative uses of information.

As firms move along the road of information mastery, they find new revelations about their customers and marketplace. Many firms were devastated to find radical differences in the reality of their customer base as compared to their perception of it prior to understanding it through a rich information environment. One high street UK bank visionary commented that shortly before a major merger with another firm their publicly stated total number of customers exceeded that of the entire population of the country. This radical difference between reality and the publicly claimed figures was a source of great embarrassment for both the firms who previously were regarded as quite sophisticated in their use of information. It was this wide gap between perception and reality that drove the evolution of a firm's focus from more administrative information to customer information. As Figure 6.13 depicts, there is a noticeable evolution of the firm's information focus as they travel down the road of information mastery.

Informational vs. operational information

As firms move along the road to information mastery, different firms approached their information mastery relative to informational

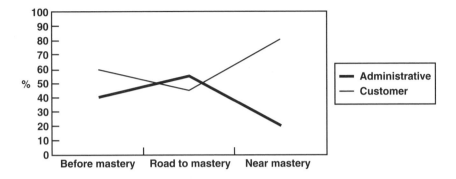

Figure 6.13   Administrative vs. customer information

information and operational information. Informational information is more of an external focus on information relative to enlightening decision-makers as to external business conditions. Informational information was predominantly customer based. Operational information is more of an internal focus on information as an indicator of the efficiency of the firm's infrastructure, e.g. distribution channel effectiveness and efficiency. Operational information was focused around distribution metrics.

The focus on informational information represented most firms' initial focus on advancing their information competency. Operational information focus tended to be more advanced and required the early learning gained from informational information to understand the idiosyncrasies of operational information.

As Figure 6.14 shows, there was a clear migration as firms became more advanced in their information competency toward a focus on operational information. In reality, the focus on operational information competency was the intertwining of the customer-focused informational information with the sophisticated understanding of a firm's operational information.

Informational information represents the next level of sophistication because it links operational dynamics with customer behavior. For example, if a customer purchases snow skiing equipment in Florida with a credit card, the operational information will indicate attributes about the item and the actual transaction, i.e. item, time of day, method of payment, and whether the item is within the customer's credit limit on this particular credit card. The informational

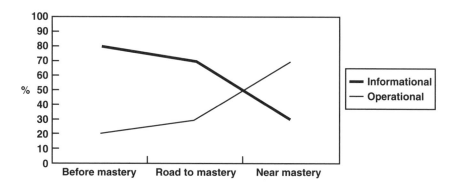

Figure 6.14   Informational vs. operational information

information would indicate attributes about the customer, and current and future behaviors, i.e. what other items in the store were purchased as an affinity relationship to this ski equipment. The informational information would also indicate the likelihood of this person procuring other goods and services related to the ski equipment. For instance, what the propensity is for this person to need to travel out of the state of Florida to use the ski equipment, e.g. rental car, plane ticket, and hotel.

Product or service/operational/consumer/financial contribution

Most firms on the road to information mastery began the slow evolution of applying consumer information more heavily than more administrative uses of information. The focus on product and service information relative to consumer and operational information gradually declined as they approached higher levels of information competency.

A further level of information competency transcended the expertise of understanding product or service flows and customer behavior to understanding these activities in the context of a financial contribution. Most firms were extremely challenged to understand the true financial contribution of specific customer behavior within specific distribution channels. Much of this was attributed to the lack of very precise measuring processes to track specific costs of specific operational processes.

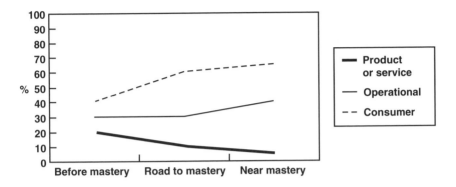

Figure 6.15   Evolution of information focus

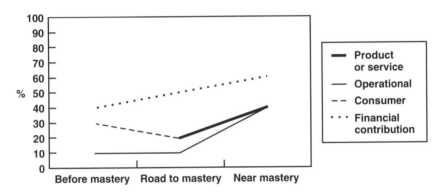

Figure 6.16   The financial contribution perspective

Information as the customer strategy

Firms that had just started their quest for a higher level of information competency delineated between information strategy and customer strategy. As firms traveled along the road to information mastery, they realized that their information strategy could not be separated from their customer strategy. In fact, a firm's information is the complete representation of their customers relative to how the firm makes its decisions.

And in all of these decisions, the firm must understand not only current customer needs and wants but also future customer needs and wants relative to their firm's operational attributes. They must also understand how any particular changes in their distribution network as well as their competitors' distribution network affects customer behavior. As one US retail visionary comments: 'it's not good enough just to open a new retail store and hope that the customers come, or just decide to close a store and hope that your best customers don't go to the competitors – you must know what your customers are likely to do when you make these operational changes'.

The firm must also understand in the context of customer behavior and distribution channels how the dynamics of pricing interact. The firms who have achieved a higher level of information competency apply microeconomics in a very sophisticated manner to how customers will behave in the future relative to the dynamics of product and service pricing for each specific distribution channel.

As firms near the levels of information mastery, they have integrated high levels of information sophistication relative to competing for a share of a customer rather than simply market share. In other words, every action they take is with an extensive knowledge of the effects and dynamics of competitor actions. The firm that approaches levels of information mastery is more attuned to the total picture of a customer's expenditures rather than just the expenditures for particular products and services. One US investment banking visionary comments that: 'We are very aggressive at pursuing information that tells us how much our customers spend with our competitors and we reward them generously for this information'. He adds: 'we also spend a lot of time asking them in their mind why they allocate their expenditures in this manner'.

Invariably, when you enter the higher levels of information competency, the sheer number of decisions increase because you are collecting and analyzing much more finite attributes of customer and distribution channel dynamics. As you go deeper into the informational detail to almost atomic levels of information, the level of operational complexity increases proportionately. This makes the complexity of corporate strategy increase proportionally as well. One UK banking visionary comments: 'as we continued to be much more sophisticated and detailed on our customer and distribution channel information we were forced to increasingly streamline the decision mechanisms within our firm'. He adds: 'We could no longer afford the time lag of decision-making as we did it under a more aggregated informational view'.

Before most firms started their journey to information mastery, their customer activities were quite basic. Most of their customer strategy was to acquire customers with little effort toward identifying and protecting their best customers as well as removing the worst customers. There was also fairly little effort toward a sophisticated approach toward migrating customers; toward further products and services; as well as toward higher profitability.

In order to discuss these different customer strategies of the masters, we can divide the actions of firms into five categories:

+ Plunder their competitor's best customers.
+ Embrace their own best customers.
+ Cultivate their high potential customers.
+ Repel their worst customers.
+ Adopt the orphans.

In the category of plunder, this is the firm's activity toward aggressively identifying and acquiring their competitor's best customers. The information master does not care about any of the other competitor's customers because it is acutely aware that if it acquires the competitor's top customers, the benefits in terms of profit and revenue will be five times as great relative to the majority of the competitor's customers.

In the category of embracing the master's best customers, this is the proactive approach to insuring that any attacks from other competitors will be met with apathy and steadfast loyalty to the master. This form of proactive protection of the master's best customers is done so by a high degree of customer understanding and need fulfillment.

In the category of cultivating the high potential customers, the master has modeled which customers have the highest potential for opportunities in cross-selling products and services as well as moving them to higher levels of profitability. The master has put in place very sophisticated processes by which these customers will be actively moved toward other products and services, which will not only generate higher value for the customers but also simultaneously create further benefits to the master. These benefits include lower attrition rates because of the broader base of product engagement, the further engagement in new product lines for the customers and ultimately a more profitable relationship with the master.

In the category of repelling their worst customers, the master aggressively repels customers that exhibited no sign of being readily moved to higher levels of product engagement and profitability. The master has created processes derived from a sophisticated understanding of how these particular customers interact to facilitate a self-initiated exodus of this customer segment to the competitor.

In the category of adopting the orphans, the master has keen awareness that as much as 30% of the market may not be patronizing any particular firm and are essentially still free agents. This requires a very sophisticated approach to model the specific attributes of this unattached segment. In many cases, this particular orphan segment can be extremely profitable.

Representative firms were asked to categorize their mix of activities within these five categories. Of these representative firms, they were asked to categorize only the categories that represented the bulk of their information initiatives. The following examples illustrate the typical mix of customer information initiatives as they evolved their information competency.

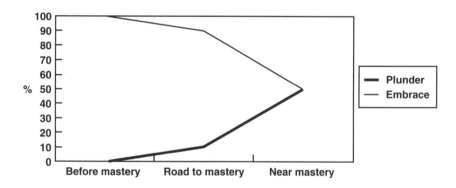

Figure 6.17   Focus on plundering and embracing customers

Plunder/embrace

As firms have traveled down the road of mastery their focus on embracing or protecting their customers became more in line with their desire to go out to and plunder or acquire their competitors' best customers. This more balanced approach appeared to be more effective in expanding their market share as well as keeping the customers once they were acquired.

Plunder/embrace/repel

In this example, firms evolved their mix by first having a fairly balanced focus on the three categories of plunder, embrace and repel. As they evolved their information competency, their efforts to embrace or protect their best customers increased. Their activities to repel their worst customers were maintained and then significantly reduced because they had extracted the bulk of the segment from their customer base. After this house cleaning took place and their information competency evolved their activities to plunder or acquire their competitor's best customers significantly increased.

The sensitivity of repelling the firm's worst customers is a very delicate issue. As firms practiced this very subtle activity to encourage the less profitable customers to leave for their competitors, they had to be very careful not to invoke a public outcry. The approach they used was very effective in that it was not an overt rejection of these less profitable customers, but more an inherent operational condition which was less favorable to customers within the segment. In other words, they embedded less inherent service and amenities in the day-to-day interactions with these customers. As customers became less enchanted with this relatively low level of service, they became increasingly susceptible to competitors' blanket incentives to attrite. As a result, they naturally left in the course of normal competitive business conditions.

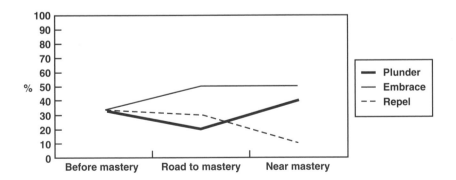

Figure 6.18   Information applied to plunder/embrace/repel

One of the sensitivities and risks involved in repelling or removing the unprofitable customers is that the firm cuts off current interactions with a customer and therefore does not have an ongoing relationship. Therefore, it is critical to do sufficient modeling to understand whether their propensity to be profitable in the future is minimal. As one US telecommunications visionary commented: 'once you get rid of a customer, they're gone'.

Another consideration for firms prior to removing certain customers is whether the firm really understands the factors surrounding this customer's unprofitability. In a large majority of the cases, it is not that the customer is genetically unprofitable, it is the fact that the firm has not designed its processes to efficiently service different customers at different cost levels. As one US banking visionary states: 'customers aren't born unprofitable, we make them unprofitable by how we serve them'.

Plunder/embrace/cultivate/repel

In this particular example, the firm initially took an aggressive stance toward plundering or acquiring their competitor's best customers and their efforts to embrace and cultivate took a lower profile. The activities of repelling or removing unprofitable customers were virtually non-existent. As they moved down the road toward information mastery, their activities to embrace or protect their best customers took a higher priority because they became increasingly aware that their best customers were being plundered by their more adept competitors. Once they felt sure that their efforts to guard their best customers were sufficient, they altered their strategy toward more of a cultivating or developing approach toward current customers. They also stepped up their activities toward removing their most unprofitable customers once they felt that their best customers were well sheltered from the continuous barrage of competitor offers.

Quality of customer information

One of the fundamental challenges early on for most of the firms seeking to improve their level of information competency was the challenge of assessing and evolving the quality of customer

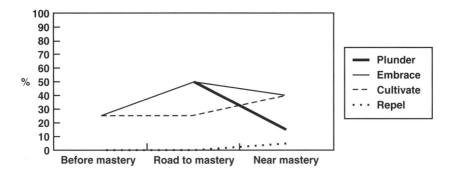

Figure 6.19   Plunder/embrace/cultivate/repel

information. Because most of the firms had operated at an aggregated or summarized level of information detail, the issues of information quality were hidden within the averages. Once the firm began their journey, and really started to dig into the detail, they found tremendous quality issues.

What most of the firms learned along the way was that they could not afford to stop all forward progress until they cleaned up all issues of quality and produced an impeccably clean information asset. They learned that there was a balance, which had to be struck between reasonable efforts toward information quality and the need to move forward in the context of an ever-changing marketplace.

One US retailing visionary stated: 'We jumped into the fray with little or no effort toward cleaning up our information quality and paid for that dearly as we tried to implement'. A US telecommunications visionary commented on how much information redundancy they had in the vast number of duplicate systems within their firm: 'The challenge of just understanding what information we had and what was completely a duplication was enormous'. He added: 'The amount of duplication shocked everyone. I think it approached 40% in terms of customer information'.

Another key issue, which seemed to be ever present, was creating one central reality for customer, operational, and financial details of the business. In reality, most firms had numerous systems, which needed to supply one central information repository. The sheer volume of keeping this central information repository updated was a massive challenge for most firms. One US retailer visionary states that: 'our biggest challenge was to convince people that our central information machine needed to be updated daily if possible'. He added: 'Our ability to serve our customers is only as good as how fresh our information is'.

Technology

Technology is the machine that enables customer information transformation. Although most firms cited the non-technological challenges as the most significant roadblocks to their success in the information race, the technological challenges are substantial in their own right. The information machines represent change to the traditional mainframe environments within the IT organizations. This proved quite challenging for many of the firms. Mainframes were designed and applied to the theories of summarizing or averaging information, long considered an acceptable business convention. The contention is that the longstanding practice of summarizing or averaging data has never been adequate although the technology to deal with anything beyond summary has not been available. Although machines are available to deal with the detail, the culture of summary is still in effect. We think in summary. We act in summary. That's why the challenge to the IT organization is significant.

First taste for the informationally starved is not enough

Many firms who had a receptive culture toward an improved information environment witnessed a phenomenon which they had not anticipated. This phenomenon occurred when an informationally starved firm was finally given adequate information. As these firms opened the flood gates to a robust information environment, their people got their first taste of what it was like to operate in a rich information environment and demanded even more detail and information. This rush of information requests precipitated by the first improvements in their information infrastructure caught most of the firms off guard. They did not expect to have such an overwhelming reception toward an asset that was previously thought of as an administrative than a value creating asset. They found their investments in the technology aspects of their information competency to be quickly engulfed by the people who had been starved of information for so long.

Early retirement of bygone systems

In hindsight, most of the firms stated that they would have more quickly retired some of the systems, which had been in place for the past decade. It was natural human procrastination that had perpetuated many of the systems' existence long after their viability had come to an end. In many cases, it was these old systems' reliability that kept them in place rather than their ability to create value from the information they housed. One US banking visionary commented: 'we should have been more proactive in putting these systems in the dumpster but culturally nobody wanted to let go of the old faithfuls, as many careers were tied to these relics'.

Part of the difficulty was that these systems were spread over multiple geographical and organizational boundaries and it was difficult to orchestrate the proactive retirement of systems which were under different business units.

Another barricade to being more proactive at retiring these older systems was the fact that most firms who were on the road to information mastery did not have complete buy-in from the entire organization as to the value of holistically moving forward as one organization.

Socialization of customer information competency to business

Many firms expressed regret that they had not dedicated more time and resources to broadly socializing the business implications of information transformation around their corporation. The more advanced firms are currently driving the use of information transformation into whatever organizations make decisions and need more detail (e.g. finance, accounting – activity-based costing). Initially, the key is to spend more resources than you think you want to spend on broadly socializing the business linkage of information transformation, while providing laser focus on one or two high payback areas.

7

Rewards of Customer Information Mastery

IT WAS CRUCIAL FOR FIRMS WHO HAD EMBARKED ON THE ROAD toward customer information mastery that there was clear evidence that this type of endeavor was worthwhile from a customer and shareholder value perspective. Therefore there was a good deal of attention paid toward projecting the payback of such an initiative before it began as well as attempting to measure the payback over the course of the transformation toward this higher level of information competency.

It was not enough for the information visionaries or champions to understand the strategic and tactical value of such a journey regardless of their unwavering belief that such an elevation of information competency would ultimately define the firm's success and destiny.

Providentially, the payback achieved by many of the firms who began to address the seven areas of information competency revealed not only how relatively primitive their proficiencies were but also that these seemingly high rewards were just a fraction of the potential payback on the road to systemic information transformation.

One of the most important ingredients for driving toward the capabilities of an information master or 'information-based competitor' is the tangible, short-term payback, which fuels long-term systemic transformation. These short-term paybacks must not be implemented separately but as part of a carefully orchestrated agenda for competing with information on a higher competitive level. The short-term payback must not be the focal point of transformation but simply the well-marketed evidence of the value of such a sustained effort.

The strength of a powerful, tenacious visionary plays a key role in payback. Their existence, or lack thereof, seems to have the most profound impact on the initial adoption of information transformation, speed of payback, and long-term magnitude of payback.

Exponential ROIs

Most firms found that early on in their endeavor to develop higher levels of customer information competency, surprisingly high return on investments were created compared to other traditional investment areas. The early projects produced return on investments within one to four years. Although the focus was not to drive short-term gains, the tactical projects, which were part of the long-term evolution, produced exponential return on investments. Many firms measured this return on investments from 20× to 40×. This was an early signal to the future information masters that the transformation of a firm's information competency held the promise of being the single most important focus a firm could have to rise above its competition.

Revenue, Cost, and Strategic Impact

The rewards from increasing a firm's customer information competency can be articulated both in traditional financial performance measurements as well as more strategic perspectives. Both perspectives are important when attempting to truly understand the business value of major information initiatives.

The combination of financial and strategic approaches for understanding and measuring the potential impact of their transformation efforts is a balanced perspective. This perspective is an equally weighted assessment of the transformation's impact on financial performance measurements as well as longer-term operationally oriented performance issues.

There is a balanced view between short-term financial approaches with the longer-term strategic approaches to give a more complete view of potential business impact. The three sections are:

1   Revenue impacts and approaches for measuring that impact.
2   Cost impacts and approaches for measuring that impact.
3   Strategic impact and approaches for understanding that impact.

Quantified Examples of Payback

Firms are focusing their information initiatives across a broad range of areas. The diverse range of areas cited by the firms is covered here together with a brief narrative for each payback area. The description is purposely brief in order to protect the individual firms and the identity of the firms.

This following compilation of payback areas cited does not reference any time frame. In contrast, the examples in the appendix focus on payback areas, which were tracked over a specific time period.

Marketing Campaigns vs. Strategic Business Decisions

The eternal struggle between tactical business initiatives and longer-term strategic initiatives produced some interesting revelations on the road to customer information mastery. Many firms who have started their journey predicted that the majority of the benefits of an improved level of information competency would emanate from tactical information-related initiatives in marketing and sales. It came as quite a surprise when the firm witnessed the tremendous value it was extracting from the new information environment relative to making better strategic decisions. When comparing the benefits which emanated from the numerous marketing campaigns and then comparing that to the benefits of improved long-term decision-making, it was clear that the benefits to long-term strategic decisions then eclipse the gain achieved by the short-term marketing campaigns.

One US retailing visionary commented that: 'We were all geared up to look for all the benefits coming from improved marketing and segmentation and then we started noticing that the information we were applying to make some of our strategic decisions far out-weighed the tactical benefits from our improved marketing campaigns'.

Many firms experienced multi-million dollar paybacks in unex-pected places. The firms whose businesses were customer intensive experienced tremendous payback at the point of contact when their employees had the information to determine the attributes of

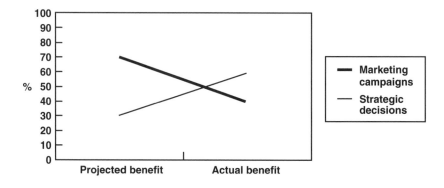

Figure 7.1   Tactical vs. strategic payback

customer profitability and act accordingly – either to increase the service level of the very profitable, or to drive mid-level customers to a higher level of profitability, or to minimize contact with customers who were deemed to be chronically unprofitable.

These paybacks not only came from understanding customer behavior more accurately but also reducing the costs associated with serving those customers. The areas which seemed most heavily influenced by increased levels of information competency lie in four primary areas.

The first was decisions to open new distribution channels, close old distribution channels, and relocate current distribution channels. The firm could perform predictive modeling that would indicate in advance which locations would prove the most efficient and effective prior to expanding any resources to build the distribution channel infrastructure.

The second was the ability to do more with less – serve more customers with fewer employees. Many employees found that because better information was more readily available, employees spent less time searching for the right information and therefore firms could employ fewer employees because of significant productivity shifts under a better information infrastructure.

The third area was the increased effectiveness of sales and marketing campaigns, which produced lower costs while achieving the same marketing successes. The firm could more accurately target a particular segment and therefore send out fewer communications or reduce the number of incentives because of truly understanding which customers needed the incentive to change particular behaviors.

The fourth area was identifying how to allocate precious customer service resources to serve the customer base relative to their desirability as customers. The firm was able to scale the largest portion of their customer service resource toward customers who represented the highest value to the firm. In several cases firms were able to eliminate entire areas of customer service simply by identifying the fact that their expenditures were being significantly underutilized. These firms detailed millions of dollars in savings as they completely shut down customer service areas which were providing little or no real value to their customers.

Managing the Movement

One of the important payback areas for many of the firms who had to manage a large group of products and assets was being able to balance the market and risk attributes of that group of products. Higher levels of information competency also produced an improved ability to view the entire group of products and the ebb and flow of products between different product categories. In many cases when a firm is selling products in a highly competitive market, a customer will buy one product and then possibly transfer to another product under a different program. The act of transferring from one product program to another product program many times is not recorded or measured and therefore suggests a successful product group when in actuality the first part group was only a temporary transition point into a second part group. The higher level of information competency gives the firm the ability to track the transitions between product groups that customers make as well as providing a true measurement of profitability as the customer moves between groups.

Understanding Special Charges to Customers

A large area of payback for most of the firms was in more effectively managing the charges that they levied on customers for base level services as well as add-on services. In most cases the income that firms received from customers would be aggregated into one success measurement without understanding the dynamics of how the charges were perceived and ultimately managed. One visionary commented that: 'we loved all the income we received in monthly charges, but we really didn't understand the dynamics of them in detail'. This visionary added: 'once we looked into the detail of these charges, we found that the local store managers were waiving a large portion of these charges for no particular business reason and we were losing all that income'. This particular firm ended up clamping down on the management of these particular charges and ended up gaining 30% more income from doing so.

Cycle Time for New Product Introduction

Another large area of payback was the added efficiency of introducing new products into a fast changing, highly dynamic marketplace. Because information was more readily available under higher levels of information competency, firms could introduce new products sometimes 30–40% faster than in their old environment. This emanated from the ability to gain access to past product launch information, up-to-date external market data, customer behavior affinities to similar products, and pricing sensitivity issues. Not only was the introduction of new products accelerated but also they were able to modify these products on the fly by having real-time market feedback. As a result, moderately successful products could very quickly be turned into highly successful products based on immediate customer response to these products.

Cycle Time to Build Technological Support Infrastructure

The cycle time for launching tactical customer information initiatives in sales, marketing, and service was radically reduced in terms of the amount of resource required to build the technological support infrastructure of the initiative. Most firms found a 10×-cycle time reduction in building the underlying technology support for such programs. The figure below depicts the average productivity gains of firms at before mastery levels of information competency compared to firms at near mastery levels of information competency.

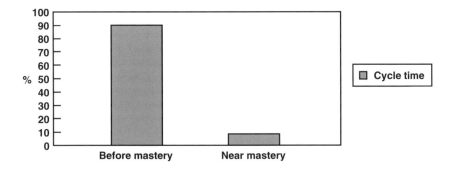

Figure 7.2   Building technological support infrastructure

Reduction in Outsourcing Requirements

One of the unexpected payback areas for many of the firms as they traveled down the road of customer information mastery was the fact that they ended up having to outsource fewer aspects of their information needs to external firms. As they grew in their understanding of the implications of a higher level of information competency, they realized that much of what they had been paying large sums of money for to external firms was now a capability which existed internally. One US investment bank visionary reflects that: 'we wouldn't think twice about writing an outsourcing check for several million dollars for information services that we now can handle internally in a matter of days'.

Reaction to Changing Business Dynamics

Another major area of payback was how quickly a firm could spot the subtle changes in the marketplace and then build a plan to adjust their business strategy. The firms that usually dominated a marketplace were the ones who were first aware of the subtle changes in such market attributes as customer behavior, price sensitivity, market share, and logistical challenges. The effects of being able to understand and address these subtle changes more quickly than your competitor not only drove revenue opportunities but also significantly reduced the costs of doing business.

Efficiency of Answering Business Questions

As businesses moved along the road of customer information mastery, they found that their overall efficiency of answering business questions improved significantly. If a firm views their business as simply a series of decisions about customers, operations, and financial matters, then the relative efficiency by which they answer those questions would have a profound impact on their competitiveness. The graph below depicts the efficiency improvements of answering business questions at different stages of information competency. Figure 7.3 illustrates how many business questions the firm can answer per fifteen hundred dollars of resource expenditure.

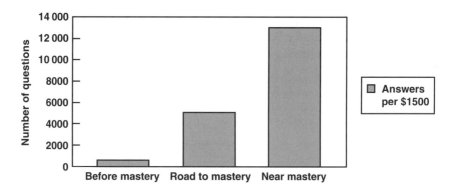

Figure 7.3   Efficiency of answering business questions

Another major payback area for firms who evolved their level of information competency was the sheer cycle time improvement of answering business questions in a dynamic marketplace. In Figure 7.4, the increased levels of information competency were shown to have a significant impact on the time required to receive answers to business questions with time compression from one hundred and sixty hours down to under one hour.

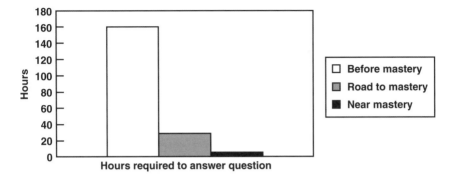

Figure 7.4   Efficiency of answering business questions – increased competency

Segment-of-One Marketing

The firms who had made significant progress on the road to customer information mastery found that their previous efforts to implement segment-of-one marketing had failed because they did not have the systemic information competency to adequately execute the promises of segment-of-one marketing. They also came to realize that as they evolved their levels of information competency, they gained the inherent capability to implement segment-of-one marketing as a competency, not a tactical business initiative – a subtle but profound distinction. One Australian banking visionary commented that: 'if we could really use our information to look into the real needs of consumers, we could experience very successful customer programs under what would typically be considered bad market conditions'.

The Process of Investing in Customer Information

The process of investing in the long-term customer information competencies, which will produce information mastery, is a delicate balance between the business functions of an organization and the technology functions of an organization. In looking at the process by which most firms invested in the initial phases of information mastery a clear pattern showed the two organizations evolving their involvement depending on which phase of the investment they were in. Most firms saw their business organizations were more heavily involved in the early stages because the catalyst behind investing was business imperatives. The technology organizations did get involved in the middle of the discovery process to ensure that there was technological compatibility with current technology infrastructure. As the information initiative evolved, the business organizations increased their involvement because of the clear business benefits that were discovered early on in the initial phases.

The impetus to invest was a mixture of external market forces as well as internal needs to increase the efficiency and effectiveness of distribution channels. Largely, the emotion which played the largest role in driving the firm's initial resource commitment was fear-based.

Most firms still went through the traditional business case process, which meant that certain corporate investment requirements were mapped. These investment requirements took the form of return on investment (ROI), return on assets (ROA), return on equity (ROE), and traditional payback calculations. Traditional hurdle rates range from 10% to 25%. Payback periods range from six months to three years. The first phase of information competency investment ranged anywhere for small initiatives of $1 million to larger initiatives of $50 million.

Payback Over Time

As the payback from the increase in customer information competency levels was tracked, most firms experienced solid proof that their investment in systemic information competency was a viable and sound decision. Although most of the payback from the early information initiatives was evident to the people closest to the initiative, the issues of executive perception and the firm's general perception required special attention. As such, these aspects of actual quantified impact and the perception of impact were monitored.

Payback Dynamics of Marketing-Focused Information Initiative #1

This particular UK bank's initiative recorded the payback dynamics of a marketing-focused information initiative over a seven-year time span. There were three key initiatives within the overall focus of following the firm's total information competency as shown in Projects A, B, and C. Project A and project B were geared more toward improvements in market segmentation whereas project C was geared more toward an improvement in marketing efficiency. As in many firms' information initiatives, the overall firm's perception of the impact of these initiatives was underestimated. This was a condition which plagued many of the firms' ability to move more quickly in terms of evolving their information competency.

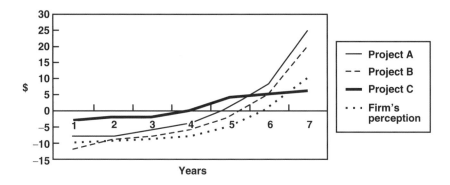

Figure 7.5   Payback dynamics of marketing-focused information initiative #1

Payback Dynamics of Marketing-Focused Information Initiative #2

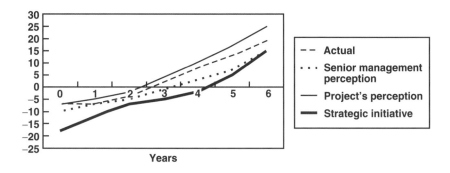

Figure 7.6   Payback dynamics of marketing-focused information initiative #2

This second example depicts a UK bank's payback dynamics of a market-focused initiative over time which details the actual quantified payback as well as the senior management perception, the project team's perception, and a representation of the longer-term strategic information transformation which was undertaken. In this example, the project team's perception of the payback actually overestimated the quantifiable payback of the primary information initiative. Senior management's perception of the impact of this information initiative was slightly below that of the actual measured payback from the initiative. The strategic evolution of the firm's overall information competency level had a slight time lag relative to the measurable marketing initiative yet was on a higher trajectory to eclipse the impact of the primary marketing initiative.

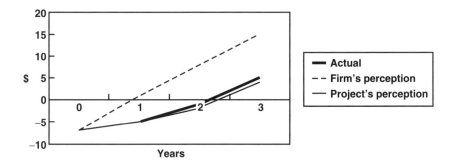

Figure 7.7   Payback dynamics of marketing-focused information initiative #3

Payback Dynamics of Marketing-Focused Information Initiative #3

In this particular example, the US banking institution's perception of the impact of the customer information initiative far exceeded that of the actual payback, which created a very dangerous environment for the future of the information initiative. While the actual impact of the primary initiative was very healthy, the exaggerated perception set a stage for possible perceived failure. The project team's perception was more in line with the actual quantifiable impact yet they had not done enough to control their firm's exuberance with the initiative's possibilities.

Payback Dynamics from Marketing-Focused Initiative Over Time #4

In this US telecommunications example, the total payback of the initiative was quite significant and on an increasing trajectory toward further payback, yet the aspects of the project which could be quantified were significantly less than those of the total initiatives impact. This was also the typical problem which plagued many of the early efforts that firms made toward customer information mastery. In most cases, the more strategic or operational-oriented impacts of an improved level of information competency were extremely difficult to place in irrefutable and rigorously quantifiable terms.

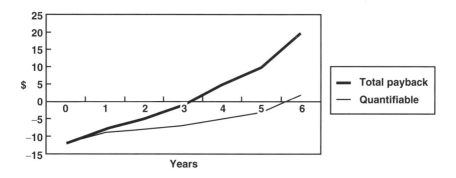

Figure 7.8   Payback dynamics of marketing-focused information initiative #4

Payback Dynamics from Marketing-Focused Initiative Over Time #5

In this US retailer's example, the firm had projected a payback which did not measure up to the actual quantified payback of the initiative. The firm's general perception of the payback fell between the quantified payback and the initially projected payback. In this scenario, the difference between projected, actual, and the firm's perceptions of the impact were in fairly close proximity to one another.

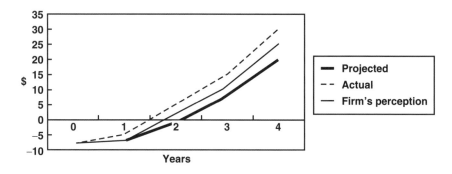

Figure 7.9   Payback dynamics of marketing-focused information initiative #5

Payback Dynamics from Marketing-Focused Initiative Over Time #6

This US bank example illustrates a market initiative that was focused on exploiting the sale of products across product groups to capitalize on product affinities. In this particular case, the actual payback from the cross-sell improvements eclipsed the perception of senior management.

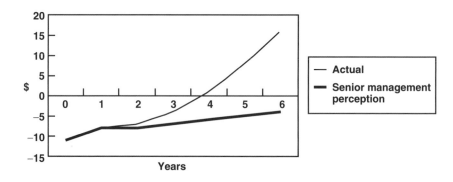

Figure 7.10   Payback dynamics of marketing-focused information initiative #6

Payback from a Credit Scoring-Focused Initiative Over Time

This US bank example illustrates the payback from the credit scoring function from a firm's increase in customer information competency. As Figure 7.11 depicts, the firm was able to proactively credit score potential customers and as a result write more profitable business while reducing their exposure to credit risk. Their investment was easily paid for in less than two years from this one small benefit area.

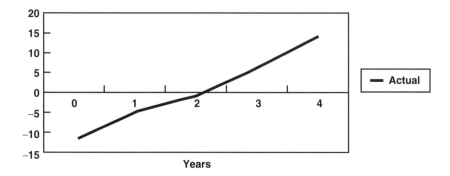

Figure 7.11   Payback timeline for credit scoring

Payback from Reducing Marketing Expenditures

This US telecommunications example illustrates a typical scenario within most of the firms in terms of the projected business case and the actual payback. Most firms experienced payback that far exceeded their original business case over the long term. There were several reasons that created this difference between anticipated impact and actual impact.

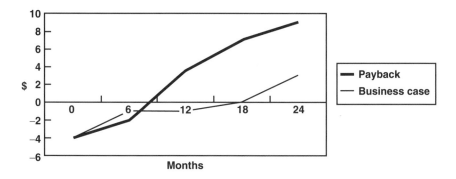

Figure 7.12   Payback timeline for marketing cost reduction

One of the primary reasons for this differential was the fact that the firms ended up improving many new areas which they had not considered in their initial estimates. In many cases, the firms reported that their focus on improving particular aspects of their customer information competency took new paths completely separate from their original plan. This situation occurred because as they learned about the unique possibilities of their own information, they dramatically changed their strategy as to where to best apply their limited resources.

Payback from a Portfolio Risk-Focused Initiative Over Time

This particular US bank decided to tackle an extremely challenging aspect of customer information competency – portfolio risk. In doing so, they pursued a path that would lead to ultimately a higher impact for their firm but would take longer to realize. They gained a tremendous amount of experience and wisdom regarding the power of information and how to apply it within their firm yet the payback for their particular project was more in the form of learning and knowledge rather than actual quantifiable changes in their risk portfolio. In hindsight, had they pursued a less challenging area such as marketing, they would have achieved a higher payback more quickly, yet they would not have ultimately achieved the same level of payback which the area of portfolio risk promised.

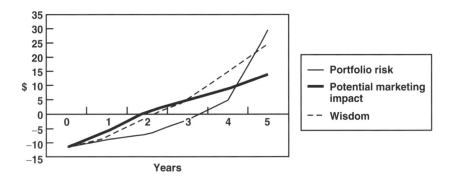

Figure 7.13   Payback timeline for portfolio risk

Payback from a Delinquency Reduction-Focused Initiative Over Time

This particular US bank had the incessant problem of attracting new business, which created a high level of payment delinquencies. As they moved to a higher level of customer information mastery, their ability to model particular attributes of a customer increased and therefore they could predict which customers had the highest likelihood of not paying. As a result they were able to achieve an eightfold return on investment on one particular product group by reducing the number of new customers that ended up not paying their bills.

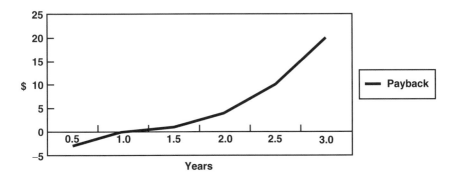

Figure 7.14   Payback from delinquency reduction

Areas of Payback in Consumer-Intensive Industries

For the firms who were traveling the road of customer information mastery, most had specific initiatives within traditional business functions. As such, the payback was tracked for a series of firms within each of these traditional business functions. There were two dimensions that were tracked for each of the primary business functions – the size of payback as well as the time it took to achieve that payback.

The two primary functional areas which were tracked, were sales and marketing as well as operations including channels of distribution.

✦   marketing;
✦   operational channels.

In addition to these specific functional areas, the performance
measurements of the profitability, payment delinquency and risk
were included.

✦   profitability;
✦   payment delinquency;
✦   risk.

The relative payback of marketing, profitability, payment delinquency,
operational channels, and risk were charted to show their relative degree of impact as well as the relative time it took to achieve the degree of
impact. It became clear that a focus on marketing had the highest impact in the shortest period of time. As a firm exploited their new-found
prowess of marketing, the levels of payback began to level off relative to
other areas of payback. In terms of profitability, the complexities were
much more involved and thus took a longer period of time to achieve
the payback, yet over the long term the high potential proved well worth
the wait. In terms of reducing delinquencies, this also had a reasonably
good payback, yet leveled off quickly as this particular aspect of information competency was brought under control. In terms of increasing
the efficiency of operational channels, this again had a higher level of
complexity to initially implement but the long-term payback was one of
the highest of all of the other areas. In terms of risk, this was very
complex as well yet did yield a significant payback over the long term.

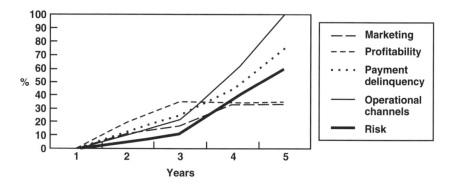

Figure 7.15   Relative time vs. size of payback

Actual Payback vs. Original Business Case

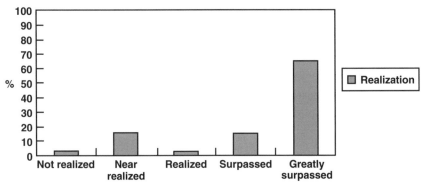

Figure 7.16   Realization of business case objectives

In terms of predicting the impact of these particular areas relative to the initial business case, most firms greatly surpassed their original business cases. A smaller percentage of the firms surpassed their original business cases and an even smaller percentage realized or achieved their business cases. The same small percentage of firms who surpassed their business cases came near to realizing or achieving their business cases. A very small percentage of firms never came close to realizing their full business cases.

Revenue Impacts from Customer Information Mastery

The revenue impacts from traveling down the road of customer information mastery come in several areas:

✦ statistical techniques enhancing customer differentiation;
✦ predicting which customers are unlikely to pay their bills;
✦ predicting which customers are likely to commit fraud;
✦ accelerating turnaround time for sales information;
✦ broadening the information view of a market opportunity;
✦ up-to-date customer information;
✦ abandoning business opportunities;
✦ accelerating turnaround time for marketing information.

Statistical Techniques Enhance Customer Differentiation

Advanced statistical techniques greatly enhance the ability for firms to differentiate their customer base. In the table below, potential customers of a major US telecommunications firm were ranked using statistical techniques. The top 10% of potential customers were scored in decile 10. For every decile the customer drops on the table, the lower the predicted behavioral scoring is for this customer sample. Each decile has the response rate for that customer sample.

Table 7.1   Statistical techniques enhance customer differentiation

	Dimension
Average response rate without statistical techniques	6.52%
Response rate of top three deciles	11.28%
Percentage increase over random	4.76%
Increase over random	73.08%
Increase in responders over random with statistics	35 733
Present value of customer response	$35
Size of marketing campaign	750 000
Expenditure per customer	$3.50
Revenue improvement with statistical techniques	$1 250 638

Decile	Predicted Score	Actual Score	Decile Lift	Cumul. Lift
10	13.41%	13.70%	2.10	2.10
9	11.79%	11.15%	1.71	1.91
8	8.80%	9.00%	1.38	1.73
7	8.40%	8.76%	1.34	1.63
6	6.10%	6.00%	0.92	1.49
5	5.50%	5.62%	0.86	1.39
4	4.80%	4.30%	0.66	1.28
3	3.70%	3.46%	0.53	1.19
2	2.40%	2.10%	0.32	1.09
1	1.00%	1.10%	0.17	1.00
Average	6.59%	6.52%	1	1

The lift in the deciles is the ratio of the response score of the decile and the average response to score of the customer sample. The lift in the deciles illustrates the enhancement that statistical techniques can provide over randomly extracting information from an entire customer base. The lift of 2.10 in decile 10 shows that there are 110% (2.1–1) more customers who would respond in this segment than in a 10% random sampling of the customer base. The cumulative decile lift illustrates the total increase anticipated when dropping below the top decile in the marketing campaign. The marketing resources may be applied more effectively when using statistical techniques such as these. This is very useful when considering that marketing departments have strict budgets and are limited in the number of mailings they may do to a particular customer base. Because the statistical techniques can answer the question as to how much better our marketing efforts do over a random sampling, the potential revenue increase can be easily calculated. The eighth decile shows a model that can produce good potential customers 72% richer than a prospect list which was generated using random techniques.

In order to show the potential revenue impact from enhanced customer differentiation, the following offers a representative example:

✦ Average response rate = 6.52%
✦ Response rate of top 3 deciles = 11.28%
✦ Present value of a response = $35
✦ Volume of promotion = 750 000
✦ Cost of individual promotion = $3.50.

The incremental improvement of the top three deciles is 4.76% or 35 733 responses (a 73% increase over random). At a present discounted value of $35 per response, potential revenues increased by $1 250 638. Under this improvement, the expenditures of implementing such statistical techniques can be recouped in one marketing campaign.

Predicting which Customers are Unlikely to Pay their Bills

Another application for applying statistical techniques is attempting to predict the likelihood of customers who have little intention of paying their bills. Applying such techniques can allow this major US telecommunications firm to direct marketing campaigns toward those customers who have a higher propensity to pay their bills. Attributes of these types of customers can be built in to statistical models very effectively. Customers who are found to have the highest likelihood of not paying their bills can then be extracted from the targeted customer group.

In order to predict which customers are the least likely to pay the following steps can be taken:

1 Determine the total target customer base.
2 Ascertain the segment of customers who are unlikely to pay.
3 Determine the amount owed in non-payment per customer.
4 Determine the degree of improvement of the target customer base.
5 Compute the total revenue recovery.

Table 7.2 Predicting which customers are unlikely to pay their bills

	Dimension
Current market revenue	2 546 000 000
Percentage of unpaid revenue	2.50%
Unpaid revenue	$63 650 000
Estimated percentage reduction in unpaid revenue	2.00%
Revenue recovery	$1 273 000

Predicting which Customers are Likely to Commit Fraud

Another aspect of this US telecommunications firm's road to information mastery is the ability to differentiate customers as to which ones are most likely to perpetrate product or service fraud through stolen phone cards, credit cards, and debit cards. Typically, the most pervasive forms of fraud that firms experience can be effectively modeled using statistical techniques.

In order to predict the impact fraud has on a firm, the following steps should be taken:

1 Determine market revenue.

2 Determine the percentage of current card fraud.

3 Estimate the potential percentage decrease in card fraud.

4 Compute the reduced revenue loss using statistical techniques.

Table 7.3   Predicting which customers are likely to commit card fraud

	Dimension
Current market revenue	$86 378 942
Percentage of fraudulent card charges	3.50%
Fraudulent card charges	$3 023 263
Decrease in fraudulent card charges	8.00%
Revenue recovery	$241 861

Accelerate Turnaround Time for Sales Information

One of the central benefits of information mastery is the improvement in market speed. How quickly this US telecommunications firm can receive, analyze, and apply sales information is the primary factor in how fast it can address sales opportunities. When a sales organization can recognize a sales opportunity more quickly than its competitors, the likelihood of dominating that market opportunity significantly increases.

In order to predict the impact of improved turnaround time for sales information, the following steps can be followed:

1 Determine the cycle time for acquiring the necessary information from such information sources as marketing, operations, billing, and customer-oriented databases.

2 Complete the separate information analysis.

3 Model the information sources and then combine them.

In one particular firm, it would take them a full twelve weeks just to perform these types of activities. As they progressed down the road of customer information mastery, the time it took to execute these same activities dropped to only six weeks – a cycle time reduction of 50%.

To determine the potential revenue impact, the following steps can be taken:

1 Capture the estimated revenue per week for Service A for a new service.

2 Capture the current time required for the current sales analysis.

3 Apply the above example for this scenario for percentage improvement.

4 Capture the weeks saved.

5 Multiply the weeks saved by the estimated revenue projection per week, and additional service implementations (Services B and C).

Table 7.4   Accelerate turnaround time for sales information

	Dimension
Potential revenue per week from Product #1	$30 000
Weeks required for sales analysis	12
Weeks required for sales analysis with higher information mastery	6
Reduction in weeks	6
Revenue increase with Product #1	$180 000
Revenue increase with Product #2	$180 000
Revenue increase with Product #3	$180 000
Revenue increase with Product #1, #2, and #3	$540 000

	BEFORE MASTERY		ROAD TO MASTERY	
Sales Analysis	Employee weeks	Actual weeks	Employee weeks	Actual weeks
Combine information sources	2	4	2	2
Information analysis	6	3	6	3
Apply models and combine	5	5	1	1
Total weeks	13	12	9	6
Productivity gains			31%	50%

Broaden the Customer Information View of a Market Opportunity

Most firms have this diversity of customer information but the information is segmented by geographical and infrastructure constraints. The information master is characterized by its ability to exploit the full value of its information without being encumbered by these non-market constraints. In doing so, they develop a better understanding of the dynamics of the opportunity. The less developed competitors may have the same number of information sources but may only apply one or two of these sources because of internal limitations.

For example, a typical firm may have the following customer information sources:

1　Primary customer systems or data warehouse.
2　Product and services systems or database.
3　Usage or distribution channel systems or database.
4　Billing systems or database.

One particular firm experienced a cycle time improvement from eight weeks to one week. In order to quantify the potential revenue improvement, the cycle time improvement of 25–60% can be used to estimate a range of similar improvements for other firms.

To calculate the cycle time's impact on revenue, the following steps are necessary:

1　Determine the product or service revenue for the first year.
2　Estimate the number of customers who would respond based on one information source.
3　Determine the percentage increase in the number of customers responding when applying multiple information sources.
4　Apply a conservative estimate of 20% increase in potential revenue.

Table 7.5 Broaden the customer information view of a market opportunity

	Dimension
Product or service opportunity per customer	$50
Number of customers buying after using one customer information source	350 000
Percentage of customers purchasing using four additional information sources	10.00%
Number of customers purchasing using four additional information sources	35 000
Revenue improvement	$1 750 000

Up-to-date Customer Information

Firms who are on the road to information mastery have a much quicker turnaround time for information which reflects the behavior of customers under particular market and economic conditions. This is critical when the dynamics of markets and customers are changing at increasing rate. Information regarding a particular market condition or opportunity is only valid if that particular market condition has not changed. It is so often the case that firms operate on old information, and therefore make inherently poor decisions. Old information can be defined from any information which is one day old to one month old – it is entirely predicated on the dynamics of market change.

To estimate the potential revenue impact, the following steps can be taken:

1 Determine the market opportunity for a product or service.
2 Determine the cycle time to analyze a market opportunity.
3 Estimate the improved cycle time to analyze a market opportunity.
4 Calculate the cycle time improvement.
5 Approximate the decrease in accuracy over a two-month period.
6 Estimate the decrease in response rate relative to decrease in accuracy.
7 Compute the decrease in response rate relative to decrease in revenue.

Table 7.6   Up-to-date customer information

	Dimension
Market opportunity during two month period	$1 500 000
Potential revenue per month	$125 000
Potential revenue per week	$31 250
Weeks required for information analysis	12.00
Weeks required for information analysis in new environment	6.00
Weeks gained from up-to-date information	6.00
Percentage decrease in information accuracy during two month opportunity	8.33%
Percentage decrease in information accuracy during analysis period	20.00%
Revenue increase from up-to-date information	$300 000

	BEFORE MASTERY		ROAD TO MASTERY	
Sales Analysis	Employee weeks	Actual weeks	Employee weeks	Actual weeks
Combine information sources	2	4	2	2
Information analysis	6	3	6	3
Apply models and combine	5	5	1	1
Total weeks	13	12	9	6
Productivity gains			31%	50%

Abandoning Business Opportunities

Many other firms commented that tremendous market opportunities presented themselves yet they knew that there was not enough resources to even attempt pursuing them. These opportunities went to competitors who had the resource bandwidth to address them. The US telecommunications firm depicted below who had a sufficient level of information mastery had fewer opportunities which they had to abandon because of lack of resources.

In order to estimate the effect of this new environment, the following steps can be taken:

1   Determine the number of business opportunities that were abandoned because of lack of information resources.

2   Estimate the business opportunities which were foregone.

3   Estimate the number of business opportunities which would have been pursued under the new environment.

4   Compute the total expected revenue.

Table 7.7   Abandon business opportunities

	Metric
Business opportunities abandoned because of lack of information resources	$1 000 000
Percentage increase in relative effectiveness of information capabilities	40%
Business opportunities which can be undertaken	$403 846

Sales Analysis	BEFORE MASTERY		ROAD TO MASTERY	
	Employee weeks	Actual weeks	Employee weeks	Actual weeks
Combine information sources	2	4	2	2
Information analysis	6	3	6	3
Apply models and combine	5	5	1	1
Total weeks	13	12	9	6
Productivity gains			31%	50%
Productivity increase			31%	50%

Accelerating Turnaround Time for Marketing Information

Many customer-intensive telecommunications firms who have increased their level of information competency find a tremendous agility in recognizing and redirecting marketing resources according to fast changing business dynamics. It is this agility that enables them to minimize their resources spent on bad promotions and maximize the resources spent on good promotions.

Many firms find that after they make a decision on a particular promotion, they are forced to follow through with a promotion until its completion regardless of its success. They are forced into this situation because they have minimal capability to obtain mid-promotion indications of success or failure.

The master's capability is that of iteration. No marketing initiative is an absolute dedication of resources. Campaigns are continually launched and proactively managed depending on the real-time success and failure of those campaigns. One particular firm indicated that over 75% of the promotion reports relative to their success and failure of a particular campaign required several weeks to process. In their new information mastery environment this firm's promotion reports are available in a matter of days, not weeks, for any given campaign.

In order to estimate the potential impact this may have, the following steps can be taken:

1 Determine the revenue loss and expenditures of a promotion which has failed.
2 Determine the revenue loss and expenditures of a promotion which has succeeded.
3 Determine the cycle time required to establish a promotion's success or failure.
4 Estimate a one-day turnaround time for promotion feedback.
5 Compute the difference in cycle time to receive feedback.
6 Compute the additional revenue gain and reduced expenditures under this cycle time improvement.

Cost Impacts from Customer Information Mastery

Information mastery has a profound effect on the operational efficiencies of firms. The following five US telecommunications examples are given to illustrate this point:

✦ marketing initiative redundancy;
✦ minimize meaningless customer contact and inducements for promotions;

◆ promotion strategy change;
◆ discontinue outmoded information infrastructure overhead;
◆ decreasing campaign size;

Table 7.8   Accelerate turnaround time for marketing information

	Dimension
Promotion #1	
Market opportunity for Promotion (#1)	$150 000
Duration in days of Promotion (#1)	45
Expenditure per day for Promotion (#1)	$1500
Total expenditure for Promotion (#1)	$67 500
Total revenue for Promotion (#1)	$9000
Revenue generated by Promotion (#1)	$405 000
Revenue minus promotion expenditures	$7500
Total effect	$337 500
Promotion #2	
Market opportunity for Promotion (#2)	$150 000
Duration in days of Promotion (#2)	45
Expenditure per day for Promotion (#2)	$1500
Total expenditure for Promotion (#2)	$67 500
Total revenue for Promotion (#2)	($1000
Revenue generated by Promotion (#2)	$45 000
Revenue minus promotion expenditures per day	($500)
Total effect	($22 500
Days required to analyze promotion	14
Days required to analyze promotion under new environment	1
Days of improved Promotion (#1)	13
Effect per day for improved promotion	$7000
Thirteen-day impact for redirected resources	$91 000
Ten promotions per year	$364 000

Marketing Initiative Redundancy

A critical aspect of any firm's marketing or sales program is to understand the boundaries of any particular campaign. There are countless examples of firms who have initiated huge marketing campaigns only to find that there is tremendous overlap between indifferent campaigns within the same firm. One particular firm initiated a multi-million-dollar direct mail campaign only to find that another group within the same firm had initiated a costly coupon incentive running concurrently in several leading magazines with the same objective. Many firms have estimated this marketing and sales redundancy ranging anywhere from 5 to 50%.

In order to estimate the impact of decreasing a firm's marketing redundancy, the following steps can be taken:

1 Choose two recent business initiatives which have redundancies.
2 Estimate the extent of the redundancy.
3 Compute the expenditures related to the redundancies.

Table 7.9 Marketing initiative redundancy

	Dimension
Marketing Initiative #1 in Segment A	475 000
Marketing Initiative #2 in Segment B	675 000
Percentage Segment A's customers that are in Segment B	12.00%
Customers who receive redundant communications	57 000
Expenditure per direct mail piece	$0.75
Expenditure per telemarketing call	$4.50
Total expenditure per direct mail piece	$42 750
Total expenditure per telemarketing call	$256 500

Minimize Meaningless Customer Contact and Inducements for Promotions

In a world of sophisticated marketing campaigns and awe-inspiring technology, most firms still have a 97% failure rate in terms of direct marketing. Not only does this cost the firm precious marketing capital for every failed contact but also the cost of incentives which have no positive impact on customer behavior.

In order to estimate the potential impact, the following steps can be followed:

1   Under the customer information mastery environment, estimate
    the improvement in segmentation in targeting incentives by
    percentage.

2   Apply that percentage improvement to the contact costs saved as
    well as the incentive costs saved.

Table 7.10   Minimize meaningless customer contact for sales inducements

	Dimension
Consumers that receive communication for inducement	300 000
Percentage of consumers who would find inducement meaningful	75%
Percentage of meaningless contacts	25%
Percentage decrease in meaningless communications	70%
Expenditure per mailed solicitation	$0.45
Expenditure per telemarketing solicitation	$4.00
Decrease in mailed solicitation expenditures per promotion	$23 625
Decrease in telemarketing solicitation expenditures per promotion	$210 000

Table 7.11   Minimize meaningless sales inducements

	Dimension
Consumers that receive sales inducement	300 000
Percentage of consumers who would find inducements meaningful	75%
Percentage of consumers who would find inducements meaningless	25%
Percentage decrease in meaningless sales inducements	70%
Sales inducement per consumer	$60.00
Decrease in sales inducement per promotion	$3 150 000

Decrease in communications and inducement expenditures	Tele-marketing	Direct Mail
Decrease in communications expenditures per promotion	$210 000	$23 625
Decrease in sales inducement expenditures per promotion	$3 150 000	$3 150 000
Decrease in expenditures per campaign	$3 360 000	$3 173 625

Decrease Expenditures by Obtaining Relevant Promotion Information More Quickly

The ability for an information master to produce the overall cost of the marketing campaigns is significant when the firm can obtain information in a real-time environment.

In order to calculate the potential marketing expenditure reduction, the following steps can taken:

1 Determine which marketing promotion has been unsuccessful.
2 Determine the expenditure per day of this marketing promotion.
3 Determine the average time required for marketing feedback.
4 Presume the new environment can obtain feedback in one day.
5 Compute the cost differential by days.
6 Compute the expenditure reduction achieved by terminating the unsuccessful campaign.

Table 7.12   Decrease expenditure by obtaining information more quickly

	Dimension
Duration of Marketing Promotion #1	45
Expenditure for Marketing Promotion #1	$3000
Total expenditure for Marketing Promotion #1	$135 000
Days required to effectively analyze sales activity	14
Days required to effectively analyze sales activity w/DataWhse	1
Decision days gained (continue/not continue) with Campaign A	13
Thirteen-day potential cost impact for Campaign A	$39 000
Ten Marketing Promotions	$390 000

Discontinue Outmoded Information Infrastructure Overhead

One of the critical elements of a firm's journey toward information mastery is the ability to discontinue as much of the outmoded information infrastructure as possible. Many firms stated that before beginning their information journey, the information redundancy was as high as 75% in their current information infrastructure. Of that 75% information infrastructure, huge costs are associated with maintaining that redundancy. In terms of information systems, each major information store can cost several thousand dollars to several million dollars per year to maintain its current state.

In order to calculate the possible impact of improved information competency, the following steps can be taken:

1   Project what percentage of current information systems can be discontinued based on the new information infrastructure.
2   Compute the expenditures associated with maintaining these outmoded information systems.

Table 7.13   Discontinue outmoded information infrastructure

	Dimension
Expenditures for outmoded Information System #1	$500 000
Information duplication in Information System #1	75%
Expenditures for outmoded Information System #2	$500 000
Information duplication in Information System #2	75%
Expenditures for outmoded Information System #3	$500 000
Information duplication in Information System #3	75%
Expenditures for outmoded Information System #4	$500 000
Information duplication in Information System #4	75%
Expenditure duplication for Information System #1	$375 000
Expenditure duplication for Information System #2	$375 000
Expenditure duplication for Information System #3	$375 000
Expenditure duplication for Information System #4	$375 000
Expenditure duplication	$1 500 000

Reducing Costs Through Reducing Marketing Volume

Using a model to select records from the prospect database can result in reduced marketing volumes and cost savings while still meeting response objectives. With an assumption for average response rate and volumes of 6.52% and 750 000, respectively, a promotion should yield 35 733 responses. However, selecting the marketing list using a model can yield similar final results with lower starting volumes. This is possible because prospect selection through modeling can generate a list with a higher response rate. An example is based upon the following assumptions:

✦ Average response rate = 6.52%
✦ Response rate of top 3 deciles = 11.28%
✦ Present value of a response = $35
✦ Volume of promotion = 750 000
✦ Cost of individual promotion = $3.50.

Improving these aspects of a firm's information competency led to a total expenditure savings of $1 108 394.

Alternative Approaches for Viewing the Impact of Customer Information Mastery

There is an eternal struggle within firms as to how to value the future impact from major customer information initiatives. Most firms attempt to measure revenue growth and cost savings as traditional areas of impact for most information initiatives. In many cases, a firm's higher level of information mastery produced benefits which revenue and cost measurements did not adequately capture. The benefits of revenue and cost address historical impacts of information mastery as they must have already happened to be measured. The fundamental problem of trying to capture the benefits of information mastery with these approaches is summed up by Dr. W. Edwards Deming's statement that: 'Management based on results is like driving a car by looking in the rear-view mirror'. There are several other approaches which are important to consider when discussing the non-traditional benefits of information mastery. These approaches are:

✦ doing it right the first time;
✦ value of future business options;
✦ risk is no longer a divine act.

Table 7.14   Reducing costs through reducing marketing volume

	Dimension
Average response rate	6.52%
Response rate of top three deciles	11.28%
Percentage increase over random	4.76%
Increase over random	73.08%
Anticipated response rate at 6.25%	35 733
Size required for response	433 316
Expenditure of decreased size of campaign	750 000
Expenditure per marketing initiative	$3.50
Total expenditure of initial marketing campaign before environment	$2 625 000
Total expenditure of initial marketing campaign in new environment	$1 516 606
Total expenditure savings from new environment	$1 108 394

Decile	Predicted Score	Actual Score	Decile Lift	Cumul. Lift
10	13.41%	13.70%	2.10	2.10
9	11.79%	11.15%	1.71	1.91
8	8.80%	9.00%	1.38	1.73
7	8.40%	8.76%	1.34	1.63
6	6.10%	6.00%	0.92	1.49
5	5.50%	5.62%	0.86	1.39
4	4.80%	4.30%	0.66	1.28
3	3.70%	3.46%	0.53	1.19
2	2.40%	2.10%	0.32	1.09
1	1.00%	1.10%	0.17	1.00
Average	6.59%	6.52%	1	1

Doing it Right for the Customer the First Time

The fundamentals of cost of quality are centered on the assumptions that work can be classified into two major categories: necessary, original work and cost-of-quality work or work that was considered secondary and non-essential. It is a necessity for a firm to be dedicated to value added work which is done correctly the first time it is attempted. The cost-of-quality work of a firm is work which was created by an earlier mistake or failure.

It is estimated that a firm can expend 25–75% of its resources in the area of cost of quality activities. In other words, a firm can expend 25–75% of its resources in correcting work that was not accomplished adequately the first time it was attempted.

One of the fundamental elements underlying information mastery is that firms have correct information the first time they attempt to acquire the information to apply to the decisions at hand. If the information is inaccurate or is unavailable, this generates additional work beyond the original task. For example, if the customer calls in to ask a question about a bill and the customer care representative gives an incorrect answer because the information that was available to them was incorrect, added work is required to correct the mistake. The cost of this person's added time as well as the customer's inconvenience is considered to be a cost-of-quality expenditure.

These cost-of-quality expenditures can take the form of avoidance, assessment, and breakdown activities. These activities are centered on resources dedicated to avoiding future problems which can arise from incorrect or inappropriate actions which had been attempted previously. Avoidance activities are centered on proactive activities which are put in place to avoid potential future problems. Assessment activities are activities which are initiated to measure the validity or accuracy of particular activities. The breakdown occurs where these activities generate internal failure which in turn generates customer service failure.

When firms have a low level of information competency and are forced to engage in a large percentage of cost-of-quality activities, those activities cost the firm in hard dollars as well as in levels of customer satisfaction and loyalty. Most firms attribute close to 50% of the cost of producing a product or service than to activities related to cost of quality.

Value of Future Business Options

Many firms commented that their new levels of customer information competency created opportunities which did not exist at lower levels of information competency. Many firms found themselves presented with new opportunities in new markets which they had no idea existed in their previous information environment. Moreover, they wouldn't have had the competency to attempt a particular market opportunity given their old level of customer information competency.

Many firms commented that particular market conditions could only be spotted when the information environment captured a certain level of detailed information about economic conditions related to customer behavior. It was this lowest level of information detail which allowed firms to recognize subtleties in customer buying behavior that indicated there may be a potential product or service opportunity underlying a particular economic condition. Once they addressed this particular market opportunity, another opportunity would avail itself within the information. It was this series of iterative opportunities that was extremely hard to predict yet happened consistently as firms evolved their level of information mastery.

Risk is No Longer a Divine Act

The issue of risk to a firm is a complex one which holds the secrets of success to many firms in many different industries. In fact, if any firm held perfect information about all risks in their business, they would be invincible. This is not possible, yet there are significant advancements being made in the areas of risk which are allowing firms to operate at fundamentally a different level.

The financial services industry is one industry which will serve as a good example as to the issues of risk and how information potentially could transform any industry or firm.

Risk plays a critical role in any industry – particularly financial services.

The risk factor in business is an area which traditionally firms have passively acknowledged without proactively attempting to manage. Much of this passive approach comes from the fact that firms have not had the level of detail to approach risk at its lowest common denominator. Much of this inability to approach risk at an atomic level comes from the lack of a systemic information competency across business units. There is also a preoccupation with the marketing and sales side of a business without a balanced attention toward the risk dimensions of higher profile sales and marketing functions.

For the firms who decided to delve into the area of risk as their first information initiative, the learning was invaluable, but the challenges were more complex than first approaching marketing or sales. Not only do they need to use the raw information for sophisticated mathematical approaches but also the firm requires an intensive framework to address risk from an extremely detailed information level.

As with attempting to initiate increased levels of information competency in more traditional business areas, the challenges of having separate business units coupled with a multitude of products and services makes the challenge of managing risk across these autonomous organizational and product entities extremely difficult. The challenge occurs when a firm is forced to assess the risk of a particular product individually without being able to look at the detailed information for an assessment based on the entire product grouping. This product grouping should have the information to support a view which allows the firm to understand the potential future loss as well as the volatility of the entire group of products. Understanding the propensity for future loss as well as the volatility must be assessed in the context of the whole.

The danger lies when a firm applies summarized and aggregated information to assess its risk. This summarized or aggregated view assumes that the group of products will have risk factors calculated on averages. In reality, an entire group of products does not perform at risk levels which were calculated at average levels of risk. The same is true when looking at specific customer groups to determine their inherent level of risk. As the level of information competency increases, firms can segment their customer groups more specifically and proactively manage them relative to their risk factors.

Another important factor of having an increased level of information competency is not only dealing with the level of risk but also when it occurs in the lifetime of the customer or product. In looking at a firm's group of customers more specifically, they can determine more precisely the timing of when risk will affect the firm. For example, the issues of when credit card customers are likely to stop paying the credit card holders is an issue which extends beyond the first year of the card issuance. The problem arises when a firm's view of risk does not extend to the entire life of the customer. For instance, if the firm's information competency level only allows them to determine the risk of non-payment in the first year that the cardholder uses the card, the view for this particular customer group may look very positive for the year. It is only in the second year in which this particular group does not pay their credit card balances that the risk will impact the firm.

The aspects of balancing the risk attributes of customer groups as well as the timing of the risk is something that higher levels of information competency embed into the firm's approach to risk. These higher levels of competency enable the firm to proactively manage the risk in the context of the group as well as when the risk is likely to impact the firm. In contrast, firms with narrower levels of information competency are forced to react to the ebb and flow of the risk dynamics of larger customer groups rather than proactively manage smaller customer groups more precisely.

Another capability which is produced when a firm travels further down the road of information mastery is the ability to price for the level of risk which it accepts in doing business with customers. Many of the firms before they started on the road to information mastery found that they could not accurately price for the level of risk that they were taking on. Not only could they not price for the level of risk but also they were taking on certain segments of customers with very high risk levels at relatively low prices. These firms also found that they were rejecting very profitable business because they could not accurately price for business which had an inherently higher risk factor. Many of these challenges were not attributed to specific analytical shortcomings but more a history of dealing with risk rather than managing risk. As one US banking visionary stated: 'the way we always had dealt with risk was that if it happens it happens and then we figured out what to do about it after the fact'.

The firms that approach near information mastery are able to acquire almost any level of customer risk because they have the underlying competency to price for that particular level of risk. One US banking visionary commented: 'now there's no such thing as a good or bad customer, just an appropriate price for that particular customer'. In very competitive markets, the firms that were near information mastery levels could more accurately price for the level of risk than their competitors. This enables them to gain up-front price advantages as well as reduce downstream costs of risk.

Another inherent problem with firms who have lower levels of information competency is that the way they measure the business does not accurately reflect the balance and timing of business risk. Many firms report on business successes in terms of revenue and profit for particular periods yet the inherent risk of the business which generated that revenue and profit may not impact that firm until the next accounting period. In other words, the first accounting period was ignoring the fact that the inherent risk would only manifest itself in the following accounting period.

8

Relative Information Mastery by Industry

INDUSTRIES HAVE DIFFERING RELATIVE ABILITIES TO APPLY information which creates an inherent cross-industry competitive advantage when a firm from the informationally stronger industry decides to dis-intermediate a firm in the traditionally information-weak industry.

This informationally based dis-intermediation is happening at an increasing rate because of the following factors:

+ globalization;
+ electronic commerce;
+ deregulation;
+ mature markets;
+ low entry barriers;
+ low exit barriers;
+ relatively weak competition.

Industries with the Most Customer Information

Certain industries' business operations have led these industries to have more customers' information reside within the industry than others have. This is not to say that the information within these industries is used effectively or efficiently. Surprisingly, the industries with typically the most customer information are the worst at applying the information.

Figure 8.1 represents four industries – financial services, retail, telecommunications, and insurance. As depicted, the financial services
industry has the most customer information. The financial services
industry is then followed by the telecommunications, retail, and
insurance respectively.

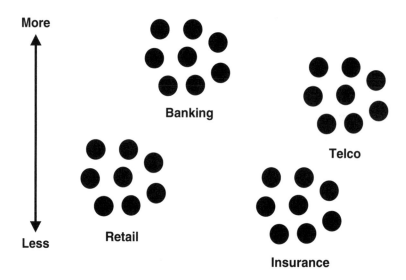

Figure 8.1   Industries with the most customer information

This figure represents an industry snapshot of the customer information yet does not show the movement toward or away from the
amount of customer information. The financial services industry is
staying relatively stagnant with a gradual move toward applying
more of their customer information. The telecommunications industry is similarly stagnant with a move toward applying its customer
information more effectively. The insurance industry is very stagnant for the most part, with little or no movement relative to the
other industries. The retail industry is making a move toward more
customer information with information vehicles of loyalty schemes,
buying clubs, and financial payment vehicles.

Figure 8.2 depicts the overall competency of an industry to apply
information in general. As the figure shows, the industries with the
least customer information have a greater ability to apply information in general. This has little or no competitive implications until

that industry decides to apply its information prowess in an informationally weak industry.

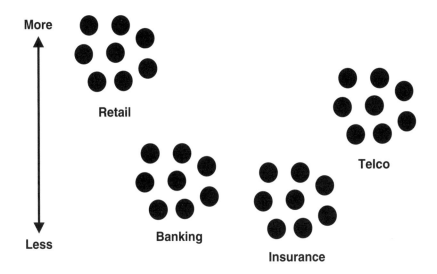

Figure 8.2   Industries' relative ability to apply information

History has shown that the telecommunications and retail industries have both made significant entries into the financial services industry.

Here are just a few examples:

1   AT&T enters credit card business, growing to $14 billion with 18 million cardholders.
2   Marks & Spencer, the UK retailer, quietly launched Marks & Spencer Financial Services Limited in 1984, growing to over 5 million cardholders, over £1.2bn in Personal Loans, and managing investments exceeding £400 million in unit trusts and tax-free savings plans (PEPs).
3   J. Sainsbury, a large UK retailer, launched their Instant Access Savings Account, paying 6.5% gross p.a. from just £1, a choice of two credit cards – the Classic and Gold Visa Cards, both linked to a Reward Card Scheme, Personal Loans, and an Options Mortgage. There are over 400 000 accounts to date.

4   Sears, the large US retailer, has a credit card business with issued cards just in 1995 of 18 million, and 6 million new cards every year, and the card business is responsible for generating a majority of the retailer's total profit.

5   Tesco, the second largest UK retailer, initially launched a loyalty card with 9.5 million current cardholders, and then entered into financial services with a card which has grown to 190 000.

6   Southland Corp., a 5400-store retail convenience store chain, with 4600 cash dispensers and automated teller machines, is now installing machines that will cash checks, and issue money orders. Their main goal is to attract people who do not have financial services relationships, i.e. to woo the unbanked.

A Glimpse of
Industry Customer Information
Competency

As we look across industries to view relative customer information competency, we see a wide variety of levels across these different industries. The levels of information competency are graphed out with the number of representative firms being listed on the x-axis and the level of information competency on a scale of 1–10 being listed on the y-axis.

The firms whose level is closer to 10 have evolved their people, process, culture, organization, leadership, information, and technology much more so than the firms who have scored closer to 1 on the chart.

Figure 8.3 indicates a firm's perception of its own information competency relative to its own industry; as the chart indicates, most firms perceived their ability to apply information as higher than it actually is.

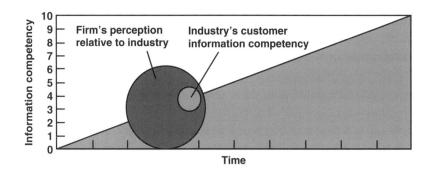

Figure 8.3 Perception of information competency

Information Competency in the Financial Services Industry

Information competency in the financial services industry has centered on two central areas – marketing and distribution. The more complex areas of profitability and risk are moving forward more slowly.

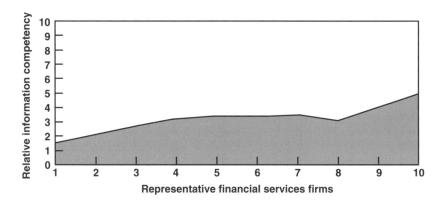

Figure 8.4 Relative information competency in the financial services industry

Figure 8.4 depicts the relative customer information competencies of ten representative financial institutions around the world. For the most part, financial institutions are relatively poor at creating significant value from the massive amount of customer information they collect in one form or another. This fact is at the core of their vulnerability as an industry. These particular firms offer a reasonable representation of the financial services industry. As the figure depicts, the majority of the firms are relatively low in information competency, with a small portion rising above the norm and only a few able to compete at a fundamentally different level. This figure is a good representation of information competency relative to the information competencies of the rest of the consumer-intensive industries (refer to graph). Some research firms believed that they were closer to achieving the levels of information competency exhibited by the top third of firms than the research found them to be. This group of firms seemed less aware of their true level of information sophistication relative to that of the research leaders. The reason for this dichotomy being that a true understanding of the potential implicit in information comes only after the firm achieves greater levels of information sophistication. Most firms in the research were humbled as they learned more about the power of information mastery. They realized how primitive their previous use of information had been.

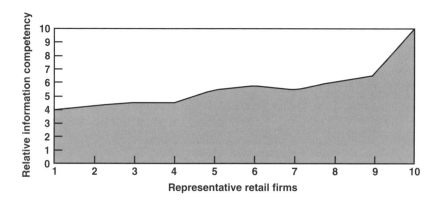

Figure 8.5   Relative information competency in the retail industry

Information Competency in the Retail Industry

For the retail industry as a whole, information competency was higher than the financial services industry. This higher competency grows out of necessity. The retail industry is far less regulated than the financial services industry, which essentially creates a competitive buffer within the industry, i.e. a competitive subsidy. The retail chart in Figure 8.5 offers a reasonable representation of the retail industry as a whole. Larger firms in the retail industry have a basic competency for moving the right goods to the right places at the right times. Only a few retailers have moved systemic information competency to a higher level of operational and customer sophistication. Their higher relative position fuels an increasing gap between the lower tiers because of greater awareness of its value.

Information transformation from a summarized and aggregated information approach brought forward the retailers' realization as to just how detached they had become from the important nuances of customers and operations.

As retailers started to close the gap between detailed reality and averaged assumptions, the retailers found huge rewards when addressing relatively small areas of their business.

The magnitude and frequency of rewards from transformation efforts from a new environment is evidence that atomic information has proven to be a central enabler for retailers beginning the information revolution. The term 'revolution' is not used lightly, nor is this the 'middle' of this revolution. We are just starting the information revolution.

The more experienced the retailers were in the use of atomic information, the more they realized how primitive they had become in truly understanding the subtleties of their business. This learning process was often humbling and painful. Atomic levels of information seem to have brought an operational effectiveness to the retailers which provides them with the opportunity for a revolutionary change as to how they conduct their business.

One retail executive very experienced in information transformation with strong payback history commented on their position in the revolution – 'So we're just really starting to tap the potential of the data'. The magnitude of rewards confirms the fact that this is the beginning of a strategic 'information transformation'.

The elements that determine retailers' information competency have some of the quintessential elements of information competency which run through all industries:

✦   one financial information reality;
✦   one customer information reality;

+ information is distribution channel independent;
+ atomic logistical efficiency (right goods/people/time);
+ information-based business initiatives are executed with no assistance from IT.

The retailer who had made the most progress has transformed their mass-market approach to a very business-oriented, easy to understand environment for all employees.

Specifically, the merchandisers are comfortable with applying the information to their procurement roles. Their comfort level has been driven from a corporate culture of expecting the merchandisers to consistently use information transformation to regularly change the way they did business.

The merchandisers also can innovatively use information to drive down the costs of their supply chain as well as doing a better job getting the right items to the right people.

The following example will appear to be fairly elementary, yet in practice for these efficiencies to reveal themselves to retailers easily and quickly is difficult to do consistently in the real world. This example is of such a competency in practice in the supply chain:

+ Compare the unit sales of each vendor's lines to identify the gross profit versus the package quantities and the turnover.
+ Develop the ability to quickly switch items from the listing of one vendor to another to get larger package quantity shipments to the store and lower their freight rates.
+ Take the remaining items from a smaller vendor and put them into the distribution center and negotiate an additional warehousing discount to move items around the distribution channel.
+ Sales are increased from better product availability – getting the right goods quicker to the right customers.

This simple information competency example drove approximately $10 million in savings on one line of goods on total net landed cost over one year.

This example was significant due to the fact that the transformation allowed the business people to execute major business initiatives without assistance from the technology group. Had this happened prior to the retailer's efforts to transform itself, there would have been major involvement from the technology group. This involvement would have demanded significantly more time and resources under the previous environment.

The US retailer's visionary commented: 'The clients (the buyers) could accomplish this all on their own . . . We (IT) weren't aware that they were working on this until after it was announced in a buying meeting'.

Dollars in the details

Most retailers' information competencies manifested themselves in a common set of payback areas:

+ promotions;
+ vendor negotiations;
+ category management;
+ seasonal merchandising;
+ ad hoc reporting;
+ sales forecasting;
+ price elasticity;
+ markdowns;
+ replenishment;
+ sell-thru;
+ assortment optimization;
+ employee hours per store.

These areas proved to be consistent payback areas for the retailers.

Again, information competency drove speed of execution. One US retailer found that when analyzing promotions, the process which previously took 5 hours, now takes 1 hour: '5 to 1' improvement in productivity. The productivity gains were one of the most surprising areas of payback for retailers. They estimate their overall productivity gains are 100% for people using the system.

These gains from having information immediately acceptable to everyone eliminated one group of keepers and distributors of information. Their motto became 'We never have to make return phone calls . . .'.

The areas such as innovation, which run across multiple categories, or the ability to attract and keep top talent, are also key manifestations of competency.

Information competency for retailers can be categorized in five basic groups:

1 Sales analysis.
2 Vendor analysis.
3 Inventory management.
4 Promotional benefits.
5 Customer profile analysis.

Very few retailers are sophisticated in the area of customer profile analysis. The degree to which retailers concentrate in these areas depends on specific corporate orientation and resource availability to truly exploit these areas.

Sales analysis

+ identification of sales' trends down to the item level;
+ identification of optimal price points by item;
+ identification of 'hot' items in time to capitalize on profits and sales;
+ identification of the downward sales trend items in time to eliminate excess stock.

Vendor analysis

+ reduced cost of goods through greater buying leverage;
+ better vendor performance due to accurate forecasts;

✦ increased profit margins via selection of high margin – high sales items;

✦ reduced out-of-stock by tracking actual vendor delivery cycles;

✦ increased stock turns through vendor partnering for just-in-time inventory.

Inventory management

✦ identification of potential stock/excess stock situations through sell-thru and rate of sales' exceptions;

✦ increasing inventory turns to reduce inventory carrying costs;

✦ supporting just-in-time inventory shipments and stocking;

✦ improved inventory forecasting at the item level;

✦ more accurate allocation of merchandise;

✦ identification of 'dead stock' to enable merchandise managers to replace it with high margin, high sales items;

✦ increased sales with the reduction of out-of-stock.

Promotional benefits

✦ mapping the best promotion type to the product at the right time and location;

✦ identifying sales impact on comparable non-promotional items;

✦ increased margins through the elimination of non-profitable promotions, advertising, and programs;

✦ more accurate forecasts and allocation based on similar promotional trends over time;

✦ support of more accurate promotional stock levels to reduce markdowns and lost sales;

✦ identifying promotional impact of affinity items.

Customer profile analysis

✦ rewarding most frequent customers with special services or discounts;

✦ profiling customer with account numbers to alert a drop in purchase behavior to allow proactive action;

✦ improving merchandise assortments to appeal to specific customer segments;

✦ providing greater convenience through services such as delivery, installation, assembly, etc.;

✦ remaining in stock for all items ordered.

Information Competency in the Telecommunications Industry

Information competency in the telecommunications industry is progressing at a reasonable pace, yet the vast changes within the industry are a distracting force to long-term information transformation efforts. As Figure 8.6 depicts, the telecommunications firms are more sophisticated than banks yet not as sophisticated as retailers are. They are still far from world class.

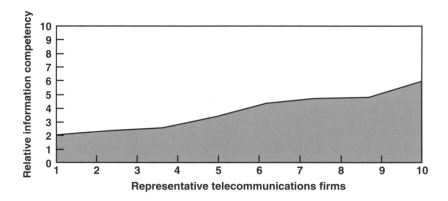

Figure 8.6   Relative information competency in the telecommunications industry

Information transformation in the telecommunications industry has had reasonable success in sales and marketing activities. As the 'Telcos' ventured into their transformation activities, they found many of their key business challenges and their corresponding drivers were favorably impacted by using information in more precise and analytical ways.

Mass-market legacies proliferate in the telecommunications industry as they have grown up during years of little regulation. In the last several decades, the regulation and resulting competitive pressures have changed dramatically. The mass-market information legacy had its roots just under a century ago when Guglielmo Marconi transmitted his first radio signals and Alexander Graham Bell invented the first telephone; no one could have imagined that one century later there would be 550 000 000 telephone users in the world.

In addition, no one could have imagined the information complexities arising from attempting to provide quality products and services to all of those global telephone users. The complexities were kept in check by strict regulation and monopolies in most areas of the world. As regulations and monopolies have become less restrictive, the importance of effective sales and marketing has increased.

Other factors such as mobile communications have also increased the need for sales and marketing. Coupling these facts with a customer environment that is roughly two-fifths nomadic, the information challenges are exponential.

These factors combined with many others have driven communications firms to place tremendous emphasis on sales and marketing activities. As a result, communications firms are looking toward information to provide the framework with which to compete with the onslaught of customer needs and competitive pressures.

The key is to apply the atomic information to specific, high value questions designed to draw out high yield answers from customer and marketing information. The focus of the benefits in the payback examples are centered around areas to increase revenues, decrease costs, and compete at more efficient operational levels.

The examples illustrate how firms in the research assessed the impact of breaking down their mass-market legacies using traditional financial performance measurements as well as strategic perspectives. The examples are a combination of traditional communications firms in the local and long distance markets.

It is important to review the major drivers of the sales and marketing function in the communications industry as well as the primary drivers of this function (customers, competition, regulation, and technology). We will also discuss key questions which provide a quick marketing information audit for current marketing information effectiveness.

The transformation of sales and marketing

In order to address the subject of information transformation for sales and marketing functions within the telecommunications industry, we must first establish a common perspective on the primary objectives of sales and marketing.

Most marketing functions' primary objective is matching customer needs with new or existing products or services. These functions must be transformed from a mass-marketing informational approach to a detailed information approach. The specific functions which must be transformed are:

1   Market research and the development of customer profiles.
2   The monitoring of customer segments and the linkage to product profitability.
3   The design of new services and re-packaging existing services.

Sales' primary objective is fulfilling needs with new or existing products. The functions supporting this objective include:

1   Selling services through telemarketing and direct sales.
2   Developing proposals based on customer specifications.
3   Providing after-sales support and maintenance of customer contact relationships.

Key business challenges and their drivers

The major drivers of the communications industry are:

✦   customers;
✦   competitors;

✦ regulation;

✦ technology.

These drivers are causing change faster than sales and marketing can effectively apply information to them.

Customers

Customers are increasingly more demanding. Customers and the factors used to segment them are changing faster than marketers are able to analyze the information and execute marketing initiatives. The trends of the future communications environment are as follows: open competition, customer-driven product offering, hyper-compression of time to market, and micro-segmentation which requires micro-segmentation profitability management. Both business and residential customers are 'informationalizing', which means seeking easier information access using the most appropriate medium (voice, data, text, and image) to the most desired location (business, home, car, and plane) on an increasingly global basis.

Competitors

There are an increasing number of alliances between previous competitors to provide seamless service. There is also an ever-increasing competitive pressure on pricing services and products. This competition comes at a time when telecommunications firms are also being challenged to control operating costs while improving quality of services and increasing revenues.

Responding to competition is taking the following approaches:

✦ reducing and controlling costs;

✦ increasing worker productivity;

✦ modernizing network infrastructure;

✦ expansion into international markets;

✦ increasing customer focus.

Regulation

Regulators at both federal and state level are encouraging increased competition in the local exchange market. Telecommunications customers are more sophisticated, with higher expectations and greater demands. Both business and residential customers are 'informationalizing', which means seeking easier information access using the most appropriate medium (voice, data, text, and image) to the most desired location (business, home, car, and plane) on an increasingly global basis. Lower regulatory restrictions are allowing flexibility in the sales and marketing function. Sales and marketing are currently experiencing increased deregulation of markets, increased segmentation, and increased competition. New product development and product push to these customers have historically been the drivers of growth. Increasingly, relationship selling is becoming a key marketing tool for the communications industry. Value added service offerings (imaging, data, etc.) are on the rise. Increasing use of direct response marketing is changing the face of sales and marketing. Cellular agent structure is being challenged as the wireless market moves toward the mass-market environment. While new services are increasingly being introduced, the focus is on increasing airtime.

Technology

The technologies which are emerging influence the ability not only to provide services but also to customize those services for individual customers. The real challenge then becomes how to predict the needs of customers relative to the utility of a particular product or service, i.e. the alignment of technology to service customers with the technology to understand customers.

The new definition of assets

The fledgling information-based competitor will need to proactively evolve their treatment of traditional assets and liabilities. This is caused by the information-based competencies shifting the actual value of traditional assets and liabilities. What was seen as a legacy firm's liability is now an information-based competitor's greatest asset. Conversely, what was once a legacy firm's most valuable asset could now be an information-based competitor's biggest liability.

This realization has led firms to rethink other aspects of the road-blocks to information competency – people, processes, organization, culture, leadership, information, and technology. For instance, what were once their most valued people skills are now their biggest burdens. What were once their most efficient processes are no longer delivering value. What were once their most effective organizational structure of command and control now makes them slow and lethargic.

In any consumer intensive industry, the retail network represents one of the most costly aspects of the business. In financial services, the branch network, once the jewel in the crown of their distribution channels, is now strangling profits. What was once a proud culture of lending, borrowing, and getting statements out on time, is now an industry under intense attack with swifter and more customer-focused players who are perfecting the art of cherry picking.

In the retail industry, major changes in urban shopping patterns have made previously profitable store locations unprofitable.

In the telecommunications industry, the infrastructure of copper wire is rapidly being considered outmoded relative to satellite and the broadband capabilities of cable companies.

As with any discussion as to the merits of infrastructure, it is largely perception. A firm's information creates that perception. The age of information has a significant impact on how a firm determines what is an asset and a liability.

The discussion of outmoded branch networks, copper wire, and passé stores is predominately an infrastructure issue. The key to the future is how accurately a firm can assess the financial merits of physical infrastructure. If the firm's ability to measure performance is limited in view and depth, the perception of a strong segment of infrastructure may be weak. In one customer-intensive industry, one large firm felt that their branch in Hollywood, California was exceedingly profitable. As they evolved their sophistication of measure, they found that the branch was the least profitable.

In the telecommunications industry, the same scenario is true for a firm's networking infrastructure. One network hub may be perceived as heavily leveraged and profitable but in fact may carry the network of unprofitable customers.

In the retail industry, the same is true for promotions. Under an unsophisticated measuring environment the promotion has appeared successful, but may have only cannibalized a more profitable product line. The future battlegrounds will be in these areas.

9

Customer Masters in the 21st Century

'As we pushed forward, and in turn, were pushed back, and then drove forward again, we entered a whole new world.'

This quote was one US retailer visionary's thoughts as they began breaking free from the shackles of their customer information legacies.

The fact that multiple firms are engaged in similar transformations raises the next daunting question for the aspiring customer information master – how fast can your firm transform itself relative to your competitors?

The definition of a customer master is as follows:

> *The customer master in the 21st century will be defined as a firm who has the ability to apply customer information at any level of granularity and in any form in order to surgically predict, act, and iterate with great speed on customer needs under the financial context of shareholder performance metrics.*

This level of customer information sophistication, which today may appear futuristic, will quickly become a competitive necessity if firms wish to achieve a leadership position.

Figure 9.1 depicts the path firms have taken as well as the path they will need to take to capture the future of customer information mastery.

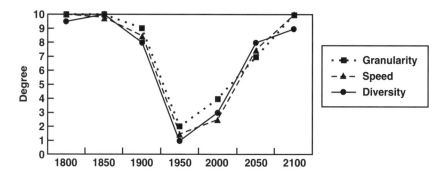

Figure 9.1   Evolution of applying information

For example, the use of binary large objects has allowed firms to record movements of human shopping patterns within retail locations. Cameras track the consumers as they walk, stop, pause, and buy. The consumer is represented as a white ghost which changes in density as the consumer lingers in front of a particular location or product. The firm can then make decisions as to how to lay out the retail location relative to a consumer's buying behavior.

The measurement of success will be taken in two primary dimensions under the context of customer and shareholder value:

1   The effectiveness to create higher relative value from information than competitors.
2   The efficiency or speed at which it creates that value.

The degree to which a firm develops these dimensions will be directly determined by the competencies of the seven principles outlined in Chapter 5 – people, processes, organizations, culture, leadership, information, and technology. In order for a firm to reach true information mastery, it must develop in all dimensions.

For a small number of firms, the efforts to develop these areas could be characterized as a race. This race is fundamentally a race back to a detailed understanding of customers, operations, and the financial performance of the firm – a race back to customer information competency.

The task of changing the mass-market legacies from over fifty years in people, processes, organizations, leadership, culture, information, and technology is daunting. New information skills must be taught to employees. New processes designed to effectively handle the lowest common denominator or atomic level of information must replace processes supported by aggregated information. Organizational structures must be designed to efficiently create value for both customer and shareholder simultaneously.

The belief system of the business information approach or information culture must be created in order for the business to believe that this atomic information approach is personally beneficial and corporately profitable. Executives must understand and believe that information is not a necessary cog but is their business in a complex world. The technology must continue to evolve to advance the insight and predictability of both customer behavior and the resulting impact to shareholders.

In the process of driving change in these areas, the areas are continuing to evolve. The future of information competency requires further development of people's skills as new types of information are captured and applied. Processes become antiquated more quickly; organizations require further changes to optimize themselves for new approaches for information sharing.

Other future short-term needs raise havoc with long-term plans for future information transformation. A successful information transformation requires a long-term commitment from executives, while simultaneously focusing on a few shorter-term objectives consistent with the overall information vision, that can be used as fuel for the longer-term challenges of the total information transformation.

Only a handful of firms truly have a strong information vision for the future backed up with the competency and will to implement them. It is those firms that have discovered that information competency is the single most important factor in determining a firm's ability to execute every core business objective. It is the vehicle upon which all other competencies travel and the conduit through which all business initiatives must pass.

The drivers that will continue to shape and define how a firm must change in order to be a successful information-based competitor are multifaceted. They will be driven equally by technology advancements as well as business imperatives which emerge as competitive necessities.

Leaders and Laggards – Attributes and Implications

The leaders who are at near customer information mastery levels are setting new levels of competitive standards for traditional business functions (sales, marketing, customer satisfaction, loyalty, distribution) primarily based on a new level of systemic customer information competency.

In most cases, competitors attribute their new found business prowess to the effectiveness of a specific business function rather than the firm's evolving systemic competency to apply customer information.

As a result, the leaders continue unfettered to reach new levels of business function competency while the laggards get unknowingly weaker as they misread both the root of their own customer weakness as well as the source of their competitor's potency.

In fact, most industries are currently undergoing tumultuous change. Once stable and profitable industries are being attacked from all angles. Pressures on margins have continually eroded.

The leaders (near customer information mastery levels)

There will be a handful of firms who will set the pace for customer information competency. Firms who compete against these customer information leaders often attribute the leader's information prowess to other areas of business acumen such as good advertising or insightful marketing managers. It is difficult to tell when firms are extremely good with information because the competency is inextricably intertwined beneath other more traditional business functions.

The leaders will typically view their customer information quest as a race rather than a journey. There is a sense of urgency about the fanatical application of information to business objectives. This is generated and perpetuated by early successes which have fueled their obsession with applying information.

In fact, the dynamics of an information master favor the leaders. As the leadership firms learn and evolve, the learning builds on itself, leading to additional transformation speed. One firm talks about its learning and how this learning continues to open up new opportunities. This UK banking visionary relates this transformation advantage:

'We climbed the first mountain, and as we looked out from our new vantage point, we could see things that were obscured to us before we had climbed that first mountain.'

Most of the information visionaries began with a base knowledge of how to move an entire organization forward in terms of their levels of customer information competency. Although they didn't have a high degree of knowledge or experience, they had the vision and drive to persevere.

Most of them had to deal with legacy cultures which inhibited the learning process itself. As they began to show early results and success from their first initiatives, the culture began to show signs of changing.

The true leaders are not touting their customer information capabilities in journals or trade publications, because they view it as their primary competitive advantage. These leaders are content for their quiet competency to be underestimated as they continue the steady acquisition of their competitors' best customers.

Of the ten representative financial services firms, there were only three which approached a customer information mastery level. One of the biggest reasons for them to actually obtain this level of information competency was the fact that they had the culture to allow the quick learning and innovation which is demanded by such a level of information competency. It is uncertain whether these three firms will obtain a higher level of information competency or drift back to the lower levels of their competitors. This high level of information competency demands continuous nurturing of the culture which is driven by the obsession with the details of customers, operations and financial attributes of the business.

The issue of whether to join others on the road of information mastery is no longer a real question for any firm who wants to still be around in ten years. The question lies in how fast a firm can travel down this road to information mastery relative to its competitors.

The changeling. The customer information master will have the unprecedented ability to change every aspect of functional areas with great speed. They have the unique ability to change products, services, customers, markets, and ultimately industries because of a flexibility which is implicit from information competency.

In a world where a firm's assets and liabilities are radically changing, firms must have this innate flexibility to interchange between the two. It will be the firm who can most quickly interchange the roles of assets and liabilities in order to take advantage of the changing market dynamics. Asked about information, there was a time when it was considered a cost or liability in terms of its role as an administrative necessity. Now it has radically changed from a liability to a strategic asset which most firms are desperately trying to evolve. The similar example is massive physical infrastructures which firms built up over the decades and are now a tremendous burden on their cost structure. Certain stores and branches in the financial services and retail industries were considered crown jewels in yesterday's marketplace, yet in today's market many are unwanted appendages which must be disposed of quickly.

The cycle time of other business activities such as mergers and acquisitions are increasingly dependent on a firm's level of customer information competency. No longer can firms pursue other acquisitions over multiple years when business conditions are changing so rapidly. One firm commented that they had just acquired one of their rivals through an acquisition which they stated that they had been pursuing for four years. At the time when they finally acquired this firm the business conditions had changed so radically that the firm's assets were no longer an asset to them but actually a severe liability.

This is particularly true when the traditional valuation of assets and liabilities are changing as quickly as markets themselves. One central asset, which seems to be consistently increasing in value, is not a firm's physical infrastructure but its information. One US bank's visionary captures this sentiment relative to assets of the future:

> '. . . when we now look at a firm in terms of their value to us, we don't look at how many buildings they own but instead how good are their customers and the information about those customers . . .'

In fact, many near-mastery firms are acquiring firms solely on the strength of their customer information. This is a growing trend for firms who have the information competency to first value a firm's customer information as well as ultimately integrate and apply it in the marketplace.

Genetic speed. The near-mastery firms inherently will have genetic speed in the marketplace – a speed that is implicit in every business function. The information-based competitor will have the unprecedented ability to accelerate and decelerate faster than its competitors.

This absolute speed manifests itself in the areas of:

+ product and service cycle time;
+ reaction to competitors' actions;
+ reaction to market dynamics;
+ reaction to customers;
+ reaction to economic changes;
+ changing itself.

Near mastery firms are experiencing improved speed in almost every aspect of their business. Not only are they able to react to competitors' attacks but also to keep abreast of all the tremendously fast changing market dynamics in their current business environment. One Australian banking visionary commented that: 'we can see that one particular area with our market was ripe for us to go after, and see it completely change over a one-week period'.

Another US banking visionary comments on their competitor's ability to compete with their level of speed:

> *'We currently run circles around them in our marketplace because they just don't have the quickness that we do in applying our customer and market information.'*

This ability to react quickly in the marketplace is being accentuated by the changes from physical distribution channels to more virtual distribution channels. Firms no longer physically interact with customers as much as they did in the past. A majority of the interaction is increasingly over the phone, Internet, and through kiosk devices. This forces a firm to have a higher level of customer information competency because there is no longer a physical person collecting physical information. The burden is now on the non-physical distribution infrastructure to capture the added information which was so naturally captured by human beings. This requires the sheer amount of information to exponentially increase. The speed at which a firm can capture this huge increase in information is critical in this new environment.

Departure from mediocrity. The customer information masters have the distinct advantage to differentiate themselves far beyond their legacy competitors. By definition, specific differentiation can only be accomplished when there is a detailed understanding of customer information regarding the targeted customer need.

In any retail-oriented industry, the more detail a firm can have regarding the customer need or behavior and the attributes of how a product or service fits that need or behavior, the more definitive the fit and resulting customer satisfaction. In the retailing industry, there is a saying that averaged or summarized information leads to average results.

In the process of examining the actual differentiation of products and services within industries, the real difference between these offerings is typically negligible. In fact, most industries could be described as a vast mediocrity relative to actual product and service differentiation.

One UK high street banking visionary openly commented that their firm:

> *'Sells exactly the same products and services as our competitors; basically they are indistinguishable.'*

This same visionary added that:

> *'Besides our product and services being indistinguishable, our level of service is almost identical as well.'*

This particular visionary sees a tremendous window for his firm to capture a larger share of their competitor's marketplace because of the low levels of information competency which seemed to be the norm in his geographic area.

He comments that:

> *'Nobody is really exceptional in the area of customer information, and our firm is poised to take advantage of that weakness in our marketplace.'*

'Information' technology. Ironically, what has been called 'information' technology has been far from its reputation. Many times, the information technology has been used to create information fortresses rather than enabling a firm's customer information. The aspiring customer information master will need to embrace the new 'information' technologies, and at the same time demand a high level of information competency.

Advances in multimedia technology will enable the advanced applications of full screen video at any customer contact point. Other uses will apply advanced computer simulations utilizing such technologies as binary large objects (BLOBS), which allow intelligent understanding of physical human behavior patterns. This BLOBS technology is used to capture video images of consumers' physical movements which are then translated into behavior patterns computers can analyze to predict consumer behavior within a physical retail space.

Information mastery will enable firms to continue to grow more powerful in their ability to process this type of customer and operational information.

High bandwidth communications will enable firms to utilize richer multimedia information environments, which will allow a more natural interface between customers and non-human contact points.

All of these new forms of information, which will be generated by the advances in multi-media technologies, will be integrated together by the customer information master.

The laggards (non-information masters)

The laggards in customer information competency will carry the burdens jettisoned by the leaders in an ever-accelerating manner. They will not benefit from the self-perpetuating success the leaders enjoy. Most importantly, they will be unknowingly left with the less desirable customers as the leaders surgically bypass and remove them.

Not only are the worst customers being jettisoned into the laggards' markets, but also the laggards are aggressively soliciting these undesirable customers. They are doing all of this with customer information inefficiencies which create inherently higher operational costs. In the words of one UK banking visionary:

> *'The worst possible situation would be the last firm in town who finds out that they have been losing all their best customers and acquiring all their competitors' worst customers.'*

The customer information master will commonly gain a clearer understanding of its competitor's customers through sophisticated modeling prior to its competitor. Conversely, the firm who understands its worst customers first has the opportunity to jettison some directly to its competitors. This scenario is occurring in most of the consumer-intensive firms. For firms, the last informationally competent firm in town will unknowingly be the sanctuary for the great 'unwanted consumer'. For the least informationally competent retailer, it will continue to support customers who only cherry pick 'loss leader' items without other profitable purchases. For the least informationally competent retailer firm, it will continue to pay unrequited premiums every time they flip-flop between carriers. It will be the firm who can predict which customers will exhibit unprofitable behavior and change their operations accordingly.

The ironic aspect of a firm not having an ability to 'see' these undesirable customers is that not only do they end up servicing these customers but also they many times aggressively solicit these undesirables. The firm with the information 'insight' can now choose not to approach the least profitable customers in the same manner in which they are able to target the most profitable customers. In a similar approach, they can create a very sophisticated method of driving marginally profitable customers toward profitability.

How to Become a Customer Information Master

Mapping a road to world-class customer information competency is somewhat like preparing to traverse a series of successively difficult mountain ranges. The previous range obscures each successive range. The subsequent ranges can only be crossed when the previous range is crossed. Subsequent ranges can only be conquered when applying wisdom from crossing the previous range.

It is clear that to be successful in moving through these mountain ranges that the seven principles of information competency must be addressed proactively. To a large extent, many of the principles should be addressed in parallel with varying degrees of intensity. The biggest danger is that firms will attempt to tackle all aspects with equal strength, which is impossible.

Each firm will have varying degrees of emphasis at various times depending on their particular environment. This is why an information competency audit is necessary to determine where the inherent strengths and weaknesses reside. The information audit can be carried out using the seven principles of information competency.

As described in Chapter 1, the fundamental 'sign posts' for the information master in the 21st century are as follows:

People

✦ Employ a balanced information mastery team.

✦ Include the following:
- people with solid history of business operations;
- people who are smart and very creative with minimal industry legacies;
- people from IT who understand the business;
- people from business who understand applying technology;
- people who can sell the potential of the new environment;
- people who have sophisticated math and statistical skills;
- people who can apply more sophisticated and iterative information in customer contact environments.

Processes

✦ Change processes to optimize creation of value from the information.

✦ Optimize processes for the lower levels of information detail.

✦ Create information flows based on information value generation.

✦ Change existing processes to reflect new decision processes optimized for information detail.

✦ Remove processes which do not support new level of information detail.

Organization

✦ Establish clear reward systems for sharing information.

✦ Identify information hoarding groups and disarm them.

✦ Establish cross-function groups specifically dedicated to information innovation.

✦ Establish explicit budgeting of cross-business unit information sharing and modeling.

✦ Create a series of information products or services for each organization.

✦ Perform regular brainstorming sessions across business units.

✦ Aggressively educate business and IT on information value.

Culture

✦ Perform an information cultural audit to determine strengths and weaknesses.

✦ Determine the information cultural alignment between business and IT.

✦ Assess the cultural residue of mass-market information legacies.

✦ Assess people's belief of the importance of information in their jobs.

✦ Align customer culture levels with information culture levels.

✦ Identify and stop superficial cultural initiatives.

Leadership

+ Identify leadership individuals who embrace the past and educate or remove them.

+ Establish clear financial rewards for information transformation short and long term.

+ Embed information directives across business functions.

+ Identify a consistent chain of information visionaries at every management level.

+ Do not attempt information transformation without a true information visionary.

Information

+ Map phases of information aggregation and begin systematic desegregation.

+ Identify where information is thrown away and examine potential value.

+ Assess percentage of known information available at point of contact and increase it.

+ Build a roadmap for evolving information quality and execute it.

+ Plan significant time to cross-match information sources.

+ Establish a roadmap for one informational 'truth'.

Technology

+ Retire legacy systems sooner than is perhaps comfortable.

+ Build an information environment which is efficient in both transaction and decision support.

+ Budget for the doubling of the primary information capabilities every two years.

+ Daily loads of all major systems.

+ Stop code develop on legacy systems.

Systemic customer satisfaction

The customer information master will need to establish a seamless stream of customer satisfaction information, which will create satisfaction, which is integral to every act of customer interface and experience.

Harking back to the earlier discussion about the historical interaction between visionaries and customers one hundred years ago, the firm of the future will interact with customers in a similar manner to the firms of the last century. The subtleties of knowing family history, emotion, facial expressions, and body language will transfer from gray matter to zeroes and ones. The burden of delivering intimacy will be placed on technology and not human thought and recollection. This level of information, which today appears futuristic, will quickly be a competitive necessity for staying in business. This information will be an integral part of understanding the intricacies of delivering higher relative customer satisfaction through what was seen one hundred years ago to be friendship-like attributes.

It has been near impossible to deliver consistent and sustainable customer satisfaction in most firms because they do not have the information required to understand and deliver products and services in the context of true customer satisfaction drivers.

The mass-market legacy firms primarily focused on product-oriented satisfaction information with minimal surveys to measure competitors' satisfaction rates. They also focus on customer satisfaction information early in the cycle of contacts rather than the latter cycles, which drive the majority of customer satisfaction. This level of capturing and applying information on customer satisfaction tends only to lead the firm toward incomplete conclusions regarding the true drivers of customer satisfaction.

The customer information master will need to measure and iterate the following details of every customer experience:

✦ accessibility of their firm;
✦ responsiveness of their firm;
✦ knowledge level of their people;
✦ promptness of their service;

✦ promises kept during solicitation and service;

✦ degree to which customers are kept informed;

✦ degree to which there is follow-up;

✦ degree to which there were no surprises;

✦ degree to which the product and /or service was right the first time.

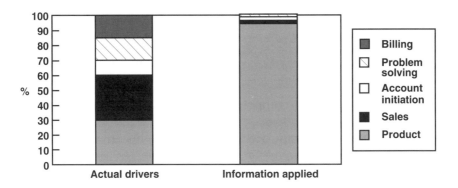

Figure 9.2   Drivers of perceived value

The customer information master also has detailed information as to their competitors' satisfaction ratings on similar products and services and in similar markets. This area of information is more complex and difficult to obtain but critical for a true understanding of relative customer satisfaction.

This point was proven during rigorous statistical research by AT&T's Bell Labs when attempting to directly tie customer satisfaction to relationship attributes of business dealings. The future viability of firms will be determined by whether those firms can apply their vast amounts of customer information in a manner that creates the attributes of a relationship when dealing with the customer, regardless of the distribution channel. The parameter for success will be the relative customer satisfaction or value as compared to competing firms or other entities. Relativity is key to the equation.

In earlier approaches, customer-satisfaction information gathered by AT&T was less relative in nature. The effects of this became known during a year when AT&T's customer satisfaction increased from 85 to 95% while their market share dropped by 6%. Impacts from this drop included laying off 26 000 employees. These market dynamics indicated that focusing on absolute customer satisfaction was meaningless in a competitive market. In reality, their competitor's customer satisfaction levels had increased beyond AT&T's and rendered their increase in customer satisfaction ineffective.

No boundaries

The customer information master will need to break every preconception about what business it is in and the respective boundaries associated with that business. If it does not break these preconceptions, their information-based competitors will.

Customer information competency is liberating in every sense of business scope and strategy. The burgeoning boundaries of traditional industry definitions are falling because information abilities transcend traditional competencies.

Having a high level of customer information mastery and the culture to implement such mastery has enabled many firms to cross the traditional industry boundaries. This has been very clear from the many examples of retail firms moving into financial services and telecommunications firms moving into financial services. The very fact that these firms could move across an entire industry boundary and compete head on with nothing but a superior competency to use customer information is a compelling statement as to the importance of a firm's relative information competency. It also illustrates that a firm not only has to look at its information competency relative to others in its industry but also their entire industry's information competency relative to the industry's information competency.

The claims that certain firms owned a leadership position within a particular industry are becoming irrelevant in a world where boundaries are dissolving every day.

This is adding to the tumultuous changes which are occurring in all industries. Industries that were traditionally stable and profitable are now under attack from all directions. Margins continue to erode as the most profitable areas of the business are 'cherry picked' by other traditional and non-traditional competitors who have higher levels of information mastery. The new levels of information sophistication have made vulnerable the dangerously small group of profitable customers which firms can not afford to be surgically cherry picked by their more sophisticated competitors. As a group, consumer-intensive firms who are not effective with their current customer information are being attacked by firms with a higher level of information sophistication and a corresponding customer-centric culture that place these firms in double jeopardy.

In the current marketplace, the competitive playing field is now around a very small group of highly profitable customers. It is the firm's ability to surgically address this very small segment of customers that will define its future relevance in the marketplace. Many firms are on a trajectory to create brilliant customer information infrastructures for their firm's future competitive advantage without the corresponding culture. This scenario will generally produce only marginally successful information competency without the corresponding culture that effectively utilizes it. Conversely, firms will ultimately fail if they have a customer-oriented culture without intensive information about the customers and operations.

Non-traditional players abound. The customer information masters are the quintessential cherry pickers of any industry. They are the ones that are breaking down the barriers which have been out for decades. Unfortunately for the financial services industry, their industry level of information mastery is relatively low when compared to the retail and telecommunications industries. As a result, they are incessantly cherry picked by those two industries. To make matters worse, once the retailers acquire the financial services customers, they can serve them more effectively and efficiently.

As one UK banking executive comments:

> *'Financial services firms are typically not customer focused; retailers are.'*

He adds: 'Why? Because we haven't had to be, until now'.

Retailers typically have become very good at placing the right products, at the right place, at the right time, to the right customers. They have had to develop a sophisticated understanding of how to use operational and logistical information to accomplish this objective. They are just now beginning to delve into the areas of expanding their knowledge of individual customers. Once they move down this path, they will be exceedingly dangerous in any industry they choose to pursue.

One US banking visionary comments that: 'the traditional financial institutions like us won't even be able to claim this industry as our own'.

He adds: 'There will be only a handful of us left who have survived, and we will have done it based on how good we are with our customer information'.

Another US banking visionary adds: 'Why will we need a separate industry such as financial services because people don't say to each other, "Let's go to the financial services industry and get some money"'.

The new chink in traditional industry armor. The future customer information masters will need to be very adept at surgically plundering and embracing the best customers, cultivating the moderately profitable customers, and jettisoning the rest. They will do this by creating very sophisticated behavioral models to understand the linkage between needs, behavior, and profitability.

Historically, the best and most profitable customers had been for the most part a corporate secret. In fact, many times the firm didn't even know which customers were most profitable. With the advent of specialized modeling tools, a leadership firm can now more effectively model the attributes of their competitor's best customers. This new Achilles' heel is quietly and quickly evolving to the point where many firms are dangerously exposed because of the razor thin number of profitable customers relative to marginally profitable customers. This cloak, which is making the best customer transparent, is disappearing.

As firms move down the road toward information mastery, the competencies of the past decades fade quickly. The hard-core marketplace tactics around plunder-and-embrace become the realities of the day. And the fact that a firm's life or death depended on a tiny segment of customers who were generating the majority of a firm's profit.

As firms travel down the road to information mastery, they soon realize just how vulnerable their business is relative to the number of customers who really keep them in business. The second realization is the fact that competitors who have a more advanced level of information competency could quite easily devastate the majority of their business just by extracting 5–10% of their customer base. After traveling down the road to information mastery one US banking visionary comments that:

> *'It was quite a culture shock for our firm to realize that only a small fraction of our customers generated the majority of our profits.'*

He adds that:

> *'. . . And on the flip side, less than 25% of our customers generate over 75% of our costs.'*

As firms travel down the road to information mastery, their ability to model which of their competitors' customers are most likely to be profitable and then quickly extract them increases their bottom line. This is changing the traditional dynamics of most industries relative to churn rates and customer loyalty. Churn rates of one decade ago are exponentially different than they are today in most industries. What were once 5% annual churn rates are now 50% annual churn rates in many industries. One UK banking visionary stated that:

> *'You better not be the last company in your industry to find this out.'*

He added:

> *'Because you'll end up with the worst customers in your industry.'*

There is a strong parallel to this in the airline industry. When one or two firms first instituted the frequent flier programs, those particular firms gained tremendous market share from those programs. As other firms entered with their flavor of frequent flier programs, the

benefits were significantly less because the programs were now a me-
too offering which generated more costs than benefits.

Legacy competition. Historically, the typical competitive scenarios
are represented by Figure 9.3. Most firms went about targeting each
other in this format. They did so in a relatively blind fashion. They
executed this scenario with relatively simple information. Each
legacy firm went after the other's customers with little or no discrim-
ination as to their relative profitability.

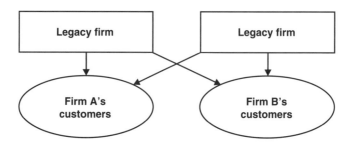

Figure 9.3   Legacy competition

Most of the efforts were geared toward acquiring customers. Surprisingly, most firms are still relatively crude at protecting and developing their present customers relative to a sophisticated matrix of
long-term profitability and propensity to attrite.

The customer information master of the future will need to evolve
far beyond this model and have a surgical precision in identifying
and acquiring their competitors' best customers. This is done by
creating mathematical behavioral models of what attributes con-
stitute a consistently profitable customer. This model will need to be
applied not only to acquiring new customers but understanding current customers' attributes of consistent profitability.

Information masters competing inter-industry. Figure 9.4 depicts the
information mastery model. The small circle in the customer oval
represented the top 10% of the most desirable customers. To identify the elite customers effectively, the information master will first
have to develop a behavior and attribute model, which can be

derived from its experience with its current customers. It can then apply that knowledge to target only the most desirable customers of its competitors. This is done through similar behavior and attribute assessment modeling. This will result in a better picture of its competitors' customers than the legacy competitor has itself.

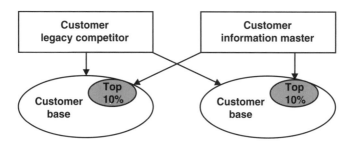

Figure 9.4   Information-based competition

The previous example illustrates the information master competing within its own industry. The likelihood of firms staying within their own industry moving forward is becoming less. Information masters are finding opportunities to expand revenue and profits in industries beyond their own. They are doing so on their own and also with compatible partners.

Death of the traditional industry. The customer information master will need to capitalize on cross-industry information models with a focus on customer share, not market share. Customer share is defined as the share that the information-based competitor can achieve across the consumer's entire spending – regardless of industry.

The customer information masters can proactively model behavior across each industry that this individual customer has dealings with.

Historically, this scenario has been extremely difficult for cross-industry efforts with traditional firms. Typically, the fear and distrust of many current cross-industry alliances keep the information sharing and integration from ever reaching full value creation. These information alliances can be described as arm's length partnerships characterized by short-term objectives and directives. They are also vulnerable to political winds from both firms.

If customers' needs are examined independently of long-standing industry definitions, the reality is that customers do not need industries. They only need products and services. Customers also do not spend their money according to industries, but only to acquire utility. This utility ranges across traditional industries, e.g. a consumer buys bread (retail), needs a checking account (financial services), and needs to communicate (telecommunications).

Firms behave as if consumers have behavior spending patterns segmented by industry. The reality is that a consumer's spending behavior in each industry is related across industries. Industry boundaries are an artificial construct of distinctively separate legacy industry models. The segmentation of market approach by industry is unnecessary in the world of the customer information master.

To graphically illustrate the absurdity of current distinctly separate industry approaches, Figure 9.5 represents the anatomical equivalent of current myopic industry approaches. Most, if not all, needs are interrelated and consequently can be linked by modeling the information captured from behavior relative to products and services.

Ultimately, retailers and communications firms will merge to focus on all aspects of a customer's life over a lifetime. This type of onslaught will be virtually indefensible by single-industry entities.

Cross-industry customer information master. Once this customer-modeling competency is developed, the information-based competitor will need to develop similar competencies, which will work equally as well in other industries. This can be done in one of two basic approaches. The first is to penetrate this new industry within the competencies of the existing firm.

Figure 9.6 shows the approach of entering an industry with no particular information alliance or partnership. What is important to notice is that in the early competitive stages, the new entrant has

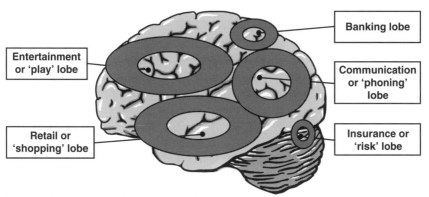

Figure 9.5 Current industry approaches

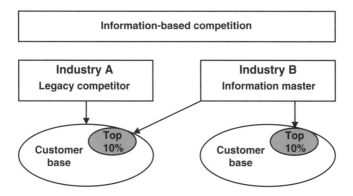

Figure 9.6 Industry entry with no information alliance

almost no vulnerability as well as little information legacies to contend with.

The other approach is to penetrate the new industry with alliance partners (e.g. Sainsbury's Bank and Bank of Scotland, Tesco and Royal Bank of Scotland, Wal-Mart and Chase). The success of both approaches will rest on the ability to apply information effectively in this new industry. In the case of the alliance approach, the success will be based on the joint ability of both firms to apply information. Much of the later approach will come down to trust between the two parties.

Conglomerate cross-industry customer information master. Another recommended information-based competition model is the conglomerate model. This is perhaps the most potent and deadly of all

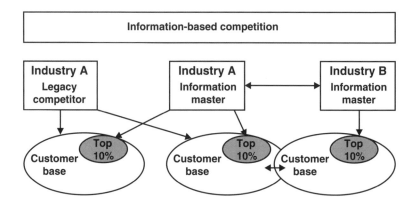

Figure 9.7   Industry entry with alliance partners

all models. They have a vast array of businesses under one roof. They are in the process of creating very sophisticated behavior models to understand and capitalize on the linkages of life events across traditional industry products and services.

As Figure 9.8 depicts, business unit A draws information from business unit B to create a better understanding of customer needs and propensity to buy products and services from both business units.

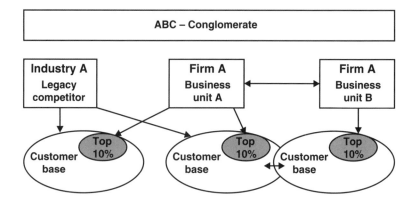

Figure 9.8   The conglomerate model

In this firm's case, their business units span almost every aspect of life's purchases. They currently have the following information sources:

+ clothing for men, women, and kids;
+ emergency road service;
+ automotive repair;
+ appliance warranty and repair;
+ home furnishings;
+ financial and credit;
+ travel services;
+ home improvement;
+ senior citizens' services;
+ dental and health insurance
+ home protection plans;
+ credit card registration services.

When the information dynamics of a multi-industry conglomerate are examined, it is evident that much of a person's life events and behavior can be tracked using the information. Currently, these types of firms are investing heavily in statisticians to understand the information they have on their customers across business units. They are attempting to understand behavior and spending patterns between business units. For example, when a person calls in to establish appliance warranties in their new home, they have the propensity to require products and services from many of these businesses.

This rich information environment is the key to the ultimate information-based competitor. The ability to predict and provide customers with precisely what they need prior to that particular life phase will place them on a different plane of competitive prowess.

The customer information master will also need to create the links between applying products and services along the life event continuum with the sustained flow of customer satisfaction indicators. They can accomplish this by creating statistical models, which correlate the purchase event with the stream of service and use events, which precede this acquisition of the product or service.

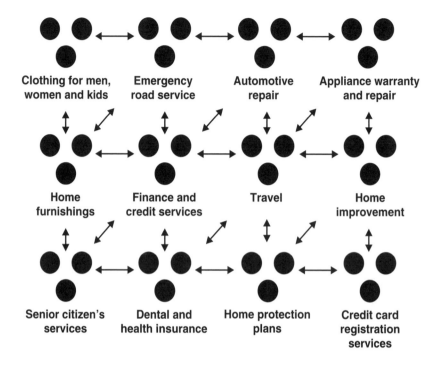

Figure 9.9   Conglomerate information flow

Another prime example of using the information advantage of a conglomerate is Virgin. Branson has managed through customer focus and branding to create successful businesses in airlines, publishing, communications, television production, and financial services.

In this environment, a customer information master could focus on top customers of each separate business unit and then model the likelihood of cross-selling products with similar acquisition attributes.

Branson has also established an alliance with Royal Bank of Scotland to launch 'One'. This financial services product offers one account, one statement, and one phone number – and all borrowings at mortgage rates. This is ideal territory for the information-based competitor.

The customer information master could examine each of its own businesses and determine what aspects of life the business unit touches. The customer behavior should then be modeled to predict the timing of life events and respective purchases. All life events carry with them specific spending and behavior patterns that can be predicted and tracked.

Regardless of approach, this information-based battleground will be waged over the same group of elite customers. It is these customers who are both the prize and Achilles' heel of any industry. The implications of these future battles are not subtle shifts in market share but the actual survival of the firm itself.

The other industry heavily involved in dis-intermediation is the retail industry. Figure 9.10 depicts an increasingly common scenario of retailers going after premium financial services' customers.

Financial services and telecommunications. This trend is continuing between financial services and the telecommunications industry. In the 1990s there was much activity in this area. The *Wall Street Journal* for 6 October 1995, reported that: 'Increasingly, the channels used by money are the same as those used for telecommunications'. It also stated that 'new technology soon may enable telecommunications companies to get around restrictions on their offering financial services'. If it is considered that the financial services' product will increasingly be digital and that the telecommunications industries' product is increasingly digital, therefore the tremendous opportunity to utilize the same infrastructure between both industries exists.

Financial services and retailers. The combination of financial services and retailers in a cross-industry partnership is an excellent opportunity to meld high frequency retail visits with the rich information sources of financial services.

Customer information masters will need to take a fresh look at new information alliances and partnerships where customers want added value and convenience. One such alliance, which has picked up speed, is the information alliances between financial services firms and retailers. The financial services firm will need partners in such alliances where information on competitors' customers is plentiful. More importantly, information partnerships are critical where the information about no-one's customers abounds.

In Figure 9.10, the financial services firm views this information alliance as one for viewing competitors' customers and more importantly the currently unattached customers or free agents. This is done by partnering with the retailer's information on its customers' shopping patterns. The customer information master in this environment would target this by applying the retailer's geographic and demographic information about their customers and map that to the financial services firm's information propensity models.

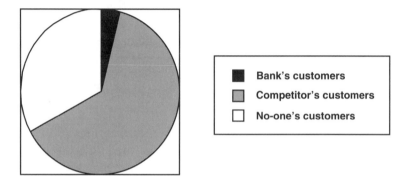

Figure 9.10   Banking's view of a retailer's customer base

This holds great opportunity in all of the following areas:

✦   drive core businesses;
✦   new markets;
✦   more customer convenience;
✦   stretch the brand;
✦   link the brand;
✦   leverage joint information;
✦   joint marketing and promotions;
✦   lower distribution cost;
✦   access to competitors' customers;
✦   access to the unclaimed customers.

Most of the alliances between financial services firms and retailers will be very important for the information-based competitor to nurture. There are a host of recent examples of financial services firms and retailers partnering although much of the partnerships are characterized by arm's length relationships. The working relationship could be categorized as that of a supplier/vendor relationship – a model the retailer is accustomed to and the financial services' person is alien to.

The customer information master should be aware of the risks of such an alliance. These risks are acutely higher when the alliance is not of the caliber of a true information-based competitor. This is the case because true business integration and value creation can only be accomplished through tightly intertwining information flows in almost every aspect of business operation and measurement.

The risks of such a relationship without tight information integration are:

+ inconsistent operational integration;
+ non-sustainable newness;
+ unmanageable profitability across the business;
+ financial risk;
+ risk to brand;
+ risk to core businesses;
+ over-supply;
+ cultural meshing.

Much of the risk of attempting this alliance without having the culture and competency of a customer information master is that the agendas of each party cannot ever rise to the ultimate win–win that joint information competency brings to the partnership. As a result, these partners have historically stayed at tactical, low value, short-term levels with each respective party operating from two distinctly different business agendas.

The attributes of the financial services' agenda relative to the retailer is as follows:

+ Have a partner.
+ Be thorough.
+ Sell products to retailers' customers.

+ Be privy to the retailer's data.
+ Have more distribution channels.
+ Sell financial services products within those channels.
+ Create new business.

The attributes of the retailer's agenda relative to financial services is as follows:

+ Have a supplier of financial services 'goods'.
+ Be fast and efficient.
+ Learn financial services.
+ Charge rent to the financial services firm.
+ Have more traffic from added convenience and service.
+ Drive core business.
+ More convenience.

It is quite clear that these types of relationships outside the bounds of the customer information master's environment are at best problematic.

In addition, these two cultures are quite different relative to their customer focus. As an informal test of each industry's customer focus, the number of times the word 'customer' was used during discussion was recorded. Retailers used the word 'customer' over twice as many times as did financial services people.

Many of the more public alliances are in the UK. Some of these include NatWest and Tesco, Royal Bank of Scotland and Tesco, Royal Bank of Scotland and Virgin, Abbey National and Safeway, and Sainsbury and Bank of Scotland. In the US there is Wal-Mart and Chase, and Bank of America and Wells Fargo have partnered with numerous supermarket chains. Most of these alliances were affected as much from the levels of regulation as they were from the levels of long-term trust which existed between them. In many cases, banks see great value in the retailer's information but retailers see little value in the bank's information and therefore only agree to share minimal information with their financial services partner.

Retailers that are banks. There are many instances where retailers quietly offer financial services within their retail operations. This has proven quite effective relative to applying information about the retail customers who have a high propensity to require financial products and services.

Several examples are Wal-Mart who retain a bank for the primary purpose of reducing the enormous clearing charges that otherwise would be charged by an external bank, Sears with their Sears National Bank, Southland (7-eleven) with their new offering of financial services through ATM networks, Sainsbury's Financial Services in the UK who offer a full line of financial services including account cards, personal loans, unit trusts and personal equity plans (PEPS), life assurance and personal pension products, Tesco Personal Financial services who also offer a full line of financial products, and Marks & Spencer also offer similar finance products and services.

Financial services, retailing, and telecommunications. The long-term goal of the customer information master is to create customer information alliances which combine the information models of multiple industries. Ideally, these alliances would take the form of actual cross-industry mergers.

One particular merger, which would be very complex and extremely difficult to compete against, would be the merger of customer information masters in financial services, retail, and telecommunications. If the individual information models are examined, there are fundamental information synergies which when brought together create a unique picture of the customer as a spending entity independent of any particular industry. In essence, it is a glimpse at the customer share, rather than the traditional market share perspective. Figure 9.11 depicts the information that these particular industries capture or have the opportunity to capture in daily operations.

The financial services industry typically captures how and where consumers spend money. The retailers typically capture what consumers purchase. The telecoms typically capture the consumer's communications, which many times are the prelude to product or service acquisition. This is only the beginning for this type of information-based competitor alliance.

If this type of partnership were brought to the ultimate conclusion of capitalizing on all information which is currently available to most firms in these industries, the ability to predict consumer behaviour would approach clairvoyancy.

All three of these industries are progressing using all the information which could possibly be captured. The banks have a multitude of additional information which passes through their operations which is either information about what, where or how.

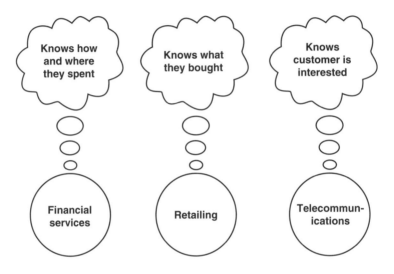

Figure 9.11   Cross-industry alliance

Privacy disarmed. The customer information master will need to disarm the legacy of applying information in the context of personal privacy. This should be done by applying more resources to capturing and modeling behavior rather than applying resources to major marketing campaigns with only a 2–3% response rate.

The firm will also need to accept the fact that information is value and that the firm will need to pay consumers for the information, which in turn will allow the firm to accurately produce the right products and services.

> *The primary reason consumers have privacy concerns is that the perception of intrusion eclipses the perceived value of the intrusion.*

The issue of privacy is clearly misconstrued by most firms. Most firms believe that most consumers get irritated by continual mail and phone solicitations yet they are willing to accept this negative reaction for the very small percentage who actually accept the solicitation.

This approach exists because firms are poor with applying information. The mantra of the future will be to focus on predicting the right product for the right customer most of the time rather than fine-tuning minute deciles of solicitation acceptances.

As such, the customers aggressively resist attempts by firms to exploit the private information to which firms, retailers, and telecommunications firms are privy. This belief will continue to be pervasive as long as customers perceive that firms use personal information with a bias toward the firm's own gain, as has historically been the case.

True value-based solicitation cannot happen until the firm has a high degree of information sophistication. The objective should be to consistently have such a compelling offering that it prompts the consumer to wait by the phone or mailbox in fear the solicitation will be missed. This thinking would be considered absurd in today's business environment, yet is not impossible to achieve with robust information regarding customer value drivers with solid mathematical approaches.

The customer information master will need to expand into every avenue of information collection including the areas of capturing physical information about movements and activities of people, automobiles, and other physical locations. Some examples of leading information usage include:

+ binary large objects used to track and analyze physical buying behavior;
+ aerial photography to determine consumer behavior relative to competitive actions;
+ satellite photography to competitors' locations.

Most firms have none of these. As a result, the crude use of information for the sole aim of driving one-way value has resulted in a bevy of privacy laws in most countries. As a result, the public expects their respective country's privacy laws to thwart the self-serving firms who seek to exploit their customer information. At the same time, firms are attempting to find innovative ways of working with their country's information privacy guidelines, usually with benefits favoring themselves.

Ultimately, the use of this customer information for the sole purpose of creating higher relative value for the customer, in concert with improving a firm's performance, is first on the agenda in the age of information. If every time a firm solicited the customer, the customer genuinely perceived that the solicitation carried a higher relative value, the customer's willingness to allow the firm to use personal information more freely would change significantly. The firms themselves created the negative perception of company-centric information use. Therefore, the burden to change this perception with a new information value approach sits squarely in the firms' court.

Firms in the research were unanimous in stating that their entrance into the age of information has caused them to rethink fundamental business operations, and indeed traditional industry processes themselves. Ultimately, firms must answer the question, 'What is it that is of real value to our firm today, which is unique and can create high relative value for customers?' The firms that have had the most progress in transforming their information legacies have the belief that the firm's most valuable asset is the most important factor in delivering higher customer value. Prior to this realization, information or data was seen as something to process – in fact, a liability or cost.

Perfect hindsight – conquering the future by looking to the past

Practice makes perfect. Perhaps the most universal comment made by those firms who had been on the road to information mastery for some time was the fact that the learning curve had been much steeper than they had expected. They had entered a new world of which they had little experience before, and really did not know what to expect when they entered. Through the trials and tribulations of learning what it meant to increase a firm's systemic level of information competency, valuable knowledge through experience was gained.

This journey took many twists and turns as the future masters wove their way through uncharted territory. This highlighted the fact that project plans should be used more as a guide rather than a step-by-step reference manual. This was evident as most firms ended up in a different place than they had planned to be.

One of the critical elements of success in a more advanced information environment was the willingness to say 'No'. As the firms evolved down the road of information competency and began to deliver a rich and robust information environment to their firms, the employees could not get enough of this new environment and demanded even more information. It was therefore incumbent on the people who were responsible for managing the information environment to develop the insight as to when the answer should be yes and no relative to added information capabilities. It was similar to that of a person being out in the desert for years and suddenly coming upon an oasis. In this case, the oasis was not filled with water but information.

As one US retail information visionary described their new environment:

> *'once we turned on the faucet of information, people just couldn't get enough, and it caused them to want even more.'*

Another US retailing information visionary commented:

> *'We gave them everything, all at one time, and everybody went crazy.'*

Another issue which came up in most firms was the deadly 'project creep'. Many of the firms set out to change their firm overnight and ended up pleasing no one because the expectations were too high.

One US retailing visionary stated that:

> *'we needed to build in short-term objectives to coincide with our long-term vision of where we wanted the firm's information capabilities to be.'*

The aspect of planning relative to building a higher level of information mastery is a critical component. One of the most challenging aspects of planning higher levels of information mastery is the fact that most teams had not had experience in this environment, and therefore to plan for this environment was filled with unknowns.

One US retailing visionary commented that:

> *'we started out with just beginning the information capability to certain parts of our distribution system, and when we were into the initiative, all distribution channels had the capability.'*

Part of the major challenge in preparing or planning for these initiatives is the level and amount of forethought that went into exactly what the firm was going to do with this type of capability once it existed.

One US retailing visionary commented that: 'after we were done with the initial phase and the employees had access to a new level of reformation, we realized that we had not involved them sufficiently in the process and, as a result, they had to go through an entirely new learning curve'.

Another aspect of forethought was the awareness of which areas were more easily addressed for establishing short-term wins. Many firms regretted tackling areas other than sales and marketing, which provided most firms with short-term wins and relatively easier implementations as a first initiative.

Another aspect of planning relative to evolving the firm's level of information competency is not only how fast to implement the new environment, but how fast to close down the old environment. Many firms had specific plans relative to implementing the new environment, but were lacking in specific plans to shut down the old environment. One US retailing visionary commented that: 'we gave people new information capabilities, but didn't have a good plan for shutting down the old stuff, and that hurt us'.

He went on to say: 'not only did we not have a plan to shut the old environment down, but we were forced to continue expanding resources to sustain the old environment much longer than we should have'.

Another challenge, which existed in planning for the new environment, was how to actually manage and maintain this new information capability once it existed. One visionary commented that: 'we had never had this level of information before and once we had implemented it, we realized that managing it required a whole new set of skills'.

Conclusion

MOST FIRMS' TRADITIONAL 'INFORMATION STARVED' BUSI-
ness functions have been suffering under a legacy of
mass-market information-oriented capabilities. Efforts to evolve
these deeply entrenched legacies have taken the form of tactical,
short-term, technology-oriented initiatives. These efforts have
accomplished little to transform the firm's systemic customer information competencies to enable an intimacy with the business once
embraced by their predecessors one hundred years ago.

Although there has been a lack of fundamental transformation,
many firms have made measurable progress in certain aspects of
information competency. While this progress has many times
yielded respectable ROIs, the fact remains that the fundamental
competency to apply an intimate knowledge of customers in the
context of their relative financial contributions is still primitive relative to what is possible.

The customer information masters must approach their business as
does Reuters; i.e. our business is information. The firms who
approach their business this way will find that everything else will
follow.

The firm who desires the status of a customer information master
must let go of the comforts of the legacies to reach this goal. To do
this, they must address the people, process, organization, cultural,
leadership, technological and informational aspects by balancing the
transitions in each category with abrupt departures from the past.
This is true for the ascent as well as reaching customer information
competency plateaus with culture stagnation. For the firm which has
reached a certain customer information competency level must let
go of some of the 'known' and 'reliable' processes in order to reach
the next level. They must be willing to take on additional corporate

risks to move to this level as well. This requires letting go of a long-proven infrastructure that may be incredibly robust but will never provide them with the information capabilities required to extend the boundaries of their competencies. The leader's bottom-line rewards come from extending these boundaries and defining new rules by which the other firms must now compete.

The race to information mastery needs to be a race back to customers. The pace of this race will be determined by firms who are operating at the fringe of innovation. The guiding light of this journey should be to create attributes of 'friendship' in their business transactions much as their forefathers did one hundred years ago.

The leading firms are, and should be, extremely quiet about their information initiatives, as there is nothing more powerful in a competitive arena. This is possible because significant advancement in information competencies is difficult to understand, making it difficult to detect. When a mastery firm attacks its competitor, the target firm does not generally attribute an information-based marketing initiative as the source of the attack.

A firm should build their entire strategy around information as their core asset. To do this successfully, the firm will need to align how its people think about, respond to, and effectively and efficiently utilize information. There must be a conscious investment both in the information competency and the change competency. A mastery firm's information competency should have two dimensions in each business strategy:

✦   to create higher relative value from customer information;
✦   to apply that information to action quicker than their competitors.

A firm's customer information competency should be the single most important factor that determines a firm's core business objectives. It is the vehicle in which all competencies travel and the conduit through which all must pass. A successful information transformation needs to have a long-term commitment from executives, while simultaneously focusing on a few shorter-term objectives which are consistent with the overall information vision, and can be used as fuel for the longer-term challenges of the total information transformation.

There are only a handful of firms in the world who are on an aggressive trajectory to evolve themselves to the status of a true information-based competitor. These rare firms have recognized the relative importance of investing beyond the enabling technologies and have started the process of investing in the other six principles which actually represent the preponderance of factors which determine a firm's ability to apply information effectively and efficiently – people, processes, organizations, leadership, information itself, and the all-important aspect of culture.

To date, the high ground for information mastery is virtually unoccupied, yet the potential remains for almost any firm to chart a long-term course for residency with the world's information elite. This course should be plotted over the long term with explicit and appropriately balanced investments in all of the seven principles of information competency with short-term, proactive touchstones of business value that are planned, measurable, and communicated.

The hardest step for any firm will be the first step on the road to information mastery – to gaze honestly into their reflection and address the realities of their greatest nemesis – themselves.

Index

Index compiled by Annette Musker